FINDING *Goodness* AGAIN

What the Book of Ruth

teaches us about

Starting *Over*

RALPH DOUGLAS WEST

BROADMAN
& HOLMAN
PUBLISHERS

NASHVILLE, TENNESSEE

Ten-Digit ISBN: 0-8054-4089-5
Thirteen-Digit ISBN: 978-0-8054-4089-8

Published by Broadman & Holman Publishers
Nashville, Tennessee

Dewey Decimal Classification: 248.84
Subject Heading: CHRISTIAN LIFE \ BIBLE.O.T.
RUTH—STUDY

Unless otherwise noted, Scripture quotations are from
the Holy Bible, New International Version, copyright ©
1973, 1978, 1984 by International Bible Society. Other
translations are identified by acronym as follows: KJV,
King James Version. NKJV, New King James Version,
copyright © 1979, 1980, 1982, Thomas Nelson, Inc.,
Publishers. RSV, Revised Standard Version of the Bible,
copyrighted 1946, 1952, © 1971, 1973.

3 4 5 6 7 8 9 10 11 12 13 14 15 12 11 10 09 08 07 06

Dedication

To Sheretta, a modern-day Ruth

Contents

Preface   ix

Acknowledgments   xv

Introduction   1

Chapter One

From the House of Bread to the Bread of Despair   5

Chapter Two

How Do You Live When You Are Running on Empty?   31

Chapter Three

The High Art of Grubbing for Grace   55

Chapter Four

The Plus Factor   79

Chapter Five

Life's Interludes of Uncertainty   103

Chapter Six
The Beginning to All God Finishes   125

Chapter Seven
A Good Faith Transaction   143

Chapter Eight
The Long, Long Corridors of Obedience   161

Conclusion   173

Preface

Mother's Day weekend was closing in on me. The week seemed to slip away like sand in a little girl's hand. Bible studies, doctoral research, writings and all were pressing me. And there I was searching for a text to preach. It appeared I had exhausted the list of Bible characters to preach as well as themes to address. It was Friday night, and I was at the NBA play-offs.

What in the name of the Bible am I going to preach?

Ruth? I have never preached her.

That's how all of this got started; I was looking for a relevant text to address the women of my congregation. As I began preaching the story of Ruth, her narrative got good to me. Also, since the previous week's sermon seemed to go over well, I thought, *Why not continue in chapter 2?* And I did, and so on the preaching went.

A few weeks into the series, I was preaching in Birmingham, Alabama, at Sixth Avenue, where my friend A. B. Sutton is the pastor. I thought I would try out the sermon idea on his congregation. After the first night a lady approached me and asked, "When are you going to write your book on Ruth?" Reluctantly I said, "I'll get to it." As I tried to brush her away she continued, "You need to write a book on Ruth." I looked back and smiled, "Yes ma'am."

Several weeks later while studying literature and theology at Cambridge and Oxford, I thought I would talk to Calvin Miller, seeing that I had his company for the summer. He immediately replied, "You need to write, Ralph. And if you're going to write you need to begin *now*. Send me a copy of your manuscript," he said, "and I'll read it and let you know what I think about it."

Simultaneously Ken Hemphill spent the summer preaching and teaching at the church, giving me a break from my weekly responsibilities. So I decided to tell Ken about this writing project that I was considering. He too encouraged me to pursue my dream and not to be deterred from it.

As the possibility of Ruth matured, I began reading more about this biblical character and the life lessons she teaches. Ruth addresses bedrock principles that you can pass on to people in need of spiritual direction. Ruth teaches us how to put life in gear and go forward with God.

Finding Fullness Again is not a commentary. There are good critical commentaries available for the curious reader. Neither is this a verse-by-verse exposition of the book of Ruth. Neither is this a book of sermons. This is an expositional narrative or a narration of the biblical story. The purpose of these writings is to allow the reader to find himself or herself in the story. However, the teachings of Ruth are not left to chance. They are clearly spelled out for the reader. No guesswork involved. This is not merely the story of Ruth because this is every reader's story.

The story of Ruth says that every person needs a new beginning. All people know something about the need to start over again. Also, every person is aware of the need to find authentic fulfillment. Which one of us has not been bombarded by advertisements telling us where we can find happiness? We all know of someone or have encountered someone who is looking for purpose in life. We know this because either we are that person or we were that person. We are searching for purpose, meaning, destiny, and love. This is what the book of Ruth revealed to me as I read her story and situated it to life.

Additionally the book of Ruth is both theological as well as ecclesiological. Theologically, the book of Ruth brings us *corum Deo,* face-to-face with the living God. Within the book we witness a God of grace and mercy on every page. We learn that nothing is left to chance as it relates to God. Continually the book reminds us that the Gracious One is with his children during life's celebrations and disappointments. Although God may appear absent he is working behind the curtains, rearranging the props for the next act in the human drama.

Ruth is also a book for the church. It speaks clearly of how the community of faith is not to prejudge and disqualify people who do not necessarily fit into our social structure. The church is to take in the Ruths of the world and let them glean in the field. The church is to provide safety, nurture, and acceptance to the people of the world. The church is to care for those the world has turned away.

Initially the book of Ruth was no more than a text to get me by Mother's Day weekend. Today Ruth has become a pastoral companion. She keeps me in touch with sensitivity. When I get too busy, Ruth slows me down to walk through the bread fields and to smell and see the fresh leftovers provided for me. When I am tired, she takes me to cool shade to lie down beneath the protection of Yahweh. When I lose loved ones she points me to Naomi. You can start over, even in the winter years of your life.

What began as a sermon has become a devotional resource for me. My prayer is that as you read this book you will have a new companion for your journey in life. Pause and reflect with this stalwart of the faith. Hear Ruth as she says, "Don't urge me to leave you or to turn back from you. Where you go I will go, and where you stay I will stay. Your people will be my people and your God my God."

Acknowledgments

Nothing worth reading is ever produced in a vacuum. The wisdom literature reminds us that "iron sharpens iron." This book is not one person's attempt to say something about Ruth that no one else has considered. At best, this is a retelling of the biblical narrative with an emphasis on starting over. The assistance of several voices already committed to the love story of Ruth has provided insight to keep this rendition on track with historical, theological, and biblical accuracy.

However, I need to applaud persons such as Al Fasol of Southwestern Baptist Theological Seminary, who read this manuscript and made technical corrections to it. Also, to my brother Ken Hemphill for believing in me and recommending this project to the patient people at Broadman & Holman. A special thanks to Calvin and Barbra Miller, who edited, typed, read, and talked me through the entire writing project. This is the second occasion that Calvin has directed me in a writing project. Thank you, Calvin, for all the unselfish time you invested in me during the writing of my first book.

To the good people at The Church Without Walls, thank you giving me the summer of 2005 to finish writing *Finding Fulfillment Again*. The summer sabbatical was time of much-needed rest. Additionally, it has been my joy and privilege to serve you as pastor/teacher for eighteen years.

Thank you, Pamela, Wanda, Macie, A. B., and Boyle for reading the unfinished manuscript and making corrections and suggestions.

A special thanks to my family. Namely to my wife Sheretta. "Ree" models what it means to find fulfillment and start over again. Thank you for being a constant source of inspiration during my pilgrim journey. And to my children, thank you for opening my eyes to see what real joy looks like. Daily you teach the old man what fullness really is. Also thank you for sharing me with so many other people that rely on my nurturing.

Finally, to the readers who have gone out full only to return empty. My hope is you will be filled anew with the Living Bread—Jesus Christ.

Introduction

Several years ago while preaching in Oakland, California, I visited my Uncle James. During my visit with him, he asked me a rhetorical question that resonates in me each time I take a book to read. "Ralph," he asked, "if you were stranded on a deserted island and had the choice of carrying three books with you, which books would you take?" The question caused me to think long and hard both theologically and philosophically. Was this a query of entrapment? Or was he genuinely interested in my literary selection?

I responded sheepishly, "I don't know. However, it seems that you have given some consideration to the question. What books would you take with you?" I asked him. Confidently he replied, "I would take a dictionary and the Bible, but I'm not sure what the third book would be." He continued elaborating on his initial question, "I would take the dictionary."

Then he added, "No person can remember all the words defined in a dictionary." Then he said this about the second book: "I definitely would take the Bible as a constant companion. No one has ever exhausted the Bible, and it would keep me reading until help arrived to rescue me."

Neither have I discovered what that third book would be. Maybe the final literary piece would be a book like the love story of Ruth, a narrative that within itself contains inexhaustible truths that will never be completely comprehended. The book of Ruth speaks of God's providentially choosing out-siders to be included in the larger scheme of his redemptive story. The story of Ruth also conveys the unique ways that God will extend his family. On the surface, the book of Ruth is a love story of an alien girl finding acceptance and hope in a land foreign to her in every way. Nevertheless, unknown to her Ruth will play a pivotal role in escorting the Messiah to the human stage.

Between meeting and marrying into Elimelech's family and giving birth to a son, Ruth will encounter death, separation, hard labor, the possibility of los-ing her chastity, as well as the probability of being redeemed by the wrong kinsman. Finally, at the birth of her son congratulations are not directed to her but to her mother-in-law. Still Ruth teaches us the valuable lesson of what it means to start over in life.

In order for persons to begin again they will need the joyful release of seeing themselves the way God sees them. In our worst moments we are never viewed by the Gracious One as insignificant.

My frame was not hidden from You
when I was made in the secret place.
When I was woven together in the depths of
the earth,
your eyes saw my unformed body.
All the days ordained for me
were written in your book
before one of them came to be."

(Psalm 139:15–16)

The miracle of salvation is not merely God saving you or me. Rather it is God's willingness to give Jesus to a world in which he knows everything there is to know about us.

At this crucial point Ruth meets us where we are, especially when so many people are unnecessarily preoccupied with their appearance. Network television is inundated with reality programming that feeds this phobia. Network program listings reveal our obsession with the superficial. Weekly shows such as *Nip/Tuck, Extreme Makeover,* and *Celebrity Weight Loss* have become the new extremes in validating the worth of people. These new-and-improved bodies are guarantees for success.

However, no amount of external reconditioning is a panacea for a deeper internal need gnawing at us.

The story of Ruth reminds us that we are more than mannequins on display and that starting over is more than cosmetics. Authentic makeover is character reconstruction. Nowhere is this truth hammered out more succinctly than when Ruth declares to Naomi, "Your God shall be my God." Although Ruth is unaware of the gamut of her statement, she moves forward in faith, a faith not completely perfected in her life. Still she takes God as her newfound token for the journey.

Chapter One

From the House of Bread to the Bread of Despair

RUTH 1:1–13

God uses the ages to redeem His creation. From Abraham to David to Jesus, there is a long umbilical cord of love. Babies from the bloodlines of grace are born one after another until the maid of Nazareth lays the choice Son of God in the manger.

The birth story sometimes takes an irregular path through the arid edges of Arabia. It is not here that our story begins, but it is through here that

it journeys. Between Joshua, the epic hero of con-
quest, and the erratic rule of Israel's first king is one
glistening stepping-stone—the book of Ruth. It is a
tale of desperation and patience, of the immortal
God and an Arab loyalist to Judah. It is a beautiful,
intriguing story of how God used human love and
new life to make a nation and ultimately to save the
world.

Before the journey begins let us set the stage
for the drama.

Born in the Breadbasket of the Near East (Ruth 1:1)

On December 26, 2004—unknown to anyone
off the western coast of the island of Sumatra or to
seismologists in observatories—the ocean surface
was shifting. Two giant tectonic plates, which had
been pushing against each other for millennia, suddenly shifted. The left plate had been sliding under
the right plate at the rate of a few centimeters a
year. But now the top plate shifted upward, lifting perhaps sixty feet along a one-thousand-mile
ridge.

Silently and undetected by scientists, geolo-
gists, or the islanders, something catastrophic was
near and about to happen. Although the Pacific
Tsunami Warning Center noticed a spike on the

seismometer, the initial reading was for an earth-quake registering 8.0 on the Richter scale. There was nothing alarming about what scientists saw on the screen on Christmas Day. In fact, the routine notice of the quake stated: "This earthquake is located outside the Pacific. No destructive tsunami threat exists based on historical earthquake and tsunami data."

It was impossible to detect any apocalyptic event occurring in such a beautiful place. It was an island where starlets, entertainers, and the wealthy went to play in the pristine surroundings. No person in Indonesia could imagine that this quiet, peaceful piece of terra ferma would be disturbed.

"Disturbed" does not quite capture the mag-nitude of what happened on that fateful day. A day after most of the visitors celebrated Christmas with family, friends, and lovers, "peace on " was about to be turned into "pain on earth." There was no time for any warning, although video cam-eras captured the approaching disaster. Tourists saw displaced trillions of tons of water in a few seconds. Silently the water pushed outward at the speed of a jet plane. Waves rose to over thirty feet in height and approached land at the speed of three hundred miles per hour. The giant wall of water claimed everything in its wake. There was nothing anyone could do as this meteorological phenom-enon was happening.

In a matter of seconds, what was once beautiful, peaceful, and bustling turned into a river of despair. The laughter of children turned into screams of fear. Lovers who were holding hands walking along the beach were separated as the raging waters divided them. One woman, a swimsuit model for the cover of *Sports Illustrated,* clung to a palm tree for eight hours. Some held on to floating mattresses, while mothers had to make the painful decision of which child's hand to hold onto and which to let go. Others who were fortunate enough to escape the water watched helplessly.

The rapid waters took over 226,000 lives. Suffering visited the luxury resorts as well as the poor fishing hamlets along the Indian Ocean coast. The tsunami changed all that encountered its force that day without regard to status, sex, age, or race. All were affected by the devastation of the tsunami. The event taught the world lessons about what is valuable to us. Sadly, some of us never learn life's valuable lesson. For instance, while many people were trying to save their lives and the lives of other people, some were more interested in their Christian Dior shirts and jewels while people were being thrown against the rocks and sharks were pushed inland.

Clearly, these people were confused, as many of us are, about life's real resources. If you assume your material prosperity is the glue that holds the pieces of your world together, it will soon fall apart. Unfortunately, we are taught from the beginning of our ability to reason that money and material goods are our security. In contrast, Ruth is a tale of high virtue. She shows that the woman who has no material prosperity may be a person of affluence. Ruth is also a guide who teaches us what to do if our plenty is reduced to poverty. Ruth teaches us how to survive when poverty invades our wealth. Ruth understood life's valuable lesson. Spiritual guidance found a way during her painful experience to identify what is important in life. Ruth teaches us how to build on these resources that we have to depend on.

Ruth also shows us that our real resources never lie in anything material. In fact, life's over-the-counter pleasures are stamped with expiration dates on them—use before thirty days. So many people today believe their real security can be found in their 401-K accounts. Others assume they will be safe if they can acquire a certain amount of financial wealth. These are prudent moves for making life enjoyable temporarily. Also, they are good investment in making life secure temporarily. But the book of Ruth unlocks ways to build your life on a solid foundation which is like building your house on rock.

If Ruth had lived in our day she would have ordered her life by one single economic plan for success. Ruth would not confuse material prosperity with spiritual wealth. Ruth's plan for success would be to "delight in the Torah of the Lord, and on His Law to meditate day and night." She was like a tree planted by the streams of water, which yields its fruit in season and whose leaf does not wither. Whatever she did prospered (Ps. 1:2–3).

Real resources do not have expiration dates stamped on them because they are never temporal. What sustains us originates from another source: "Now we know that if the earthly tent we live in is destroyed, we have a building from God, an eternal house in heaven, not built by human hands" (2 Cor. 5:1). Ruth may preach to us that the one way to determine whether we have authentic, sufficient life is to ask, Can my assets be manufactured by people? If so, they are not bona fide security. If what you call real resources are ageless gifts given to us by God the Father (forgiveness, grace, mercy, and redemption), then you have the real thing.

Ruth personifies the conclusion of the Sermon on the Mount a thousand years before it was written. Build your life on the rock. When the rains and the floods beat against your life, it will not collapse. These resources prepare us for temporal resources and teach us how to use them according to God's design.

There is nothing inherently evil in material wealth, just as there is nothing implicitly virtuous in poverty. Material things are gifts, and they should never be treated as anything other than that. Keep in mind the central truth by which Ruth lived: Life deals harshly with anyone who substitutes material possessions for spiritual vitality.

This can especially happen when we have a need that only the resource of friendship can supply. Ruth and her mother-in-law exemplified what the philosopher Aristotle said about friendship: "A friend is a single soul dwelling in two bodies." Consequently when a friend declares himself your confidant, you have the tendency to trust his verbal commitment interminably. Because of the truth in this declaration, a good friend comes in a time of need to be a friend who fulfills his pledge of fidelity: "I will be there for you in your time of need." Unfortunately, many friendships are no more than acquaintances shrouded in the garments of shallow caprice. As long as you satisfy the pathetic requirements of these insecure, self-absorbed, egomaniacal people, they'll be there. But the moment you no longer perform according to their whims and wishes, you are discarded. This is a theme many people know all too well.

- When these so-called friends turn their backs on our needs, we feel used.
- When these bogus friends turn their backs on our needs, we feel sick.
- When Iscariots turn their backs on our needs, we feel angry.

- When these Benedict Arnolds turn their backs on our needs, we feel bitter.

The psalmist felt the sting of such betrayal when he wrote, "Even my close friend, whom I trusted, he who shared my bread, has lifted up his heel against me" (Ps. 41:9).

The reason for our pain in friendship is that we made these people our ultimate resource in our time of need. But we find in our self-made proverbs a word of wisdom: If you want to have a friend you must first show yourself friendly. Then you will know that "a man of many companions may come to ruin, but there is a friend who sticks closer than a brother" (Prov. 18:24). It is in Jesus Christ that we are guaranteed the real worth of friendship. "Greater love has no one than this, that he lay down his life for his friends. You are my friends if you do what I command" (John 15:13–14). This is a friend who will never turn his back on us in our time of need.

Elimelech Breadbasket

The opening line of the story of Ruth begins, "There was a famine in the land." The generosity of God is our provision once we find ourselves in exile from the land of bread.

As a resident of Bethlehem, Elimelech, Naomi's husband, knew this was the one place he could find food for his family. But he found himself face-to-face with a need that no material resource or human resource could satisfy. Now Elimelech had to make a hard choice—whether to stay in Bethlehem, a bread-basket with no granary, or to relocate the family clan to a place that appeared to offer a better life. He could stay in Bethlehem and possibly starve, or he could seek greener pastures and wait until the famine was over. Or he could move his family to some other place. Wherever he moved, he would be an alien, or foreigner. Maybe his choice to relocate was influenced by the fact that this famine hit when there was no king, and the people were left to their own leadership. As a stranger in someone else's town, he placed himself at their mercy. If his next stop was Moab, he would be at the mercy of the Moabites.

Elimelech was a father, and he had to take care of his family. He would rather steal than let his family starve. What parent wouldn't go to extremes to provide for his or her family? The spiritual and moral role of a father is to serve his family as priest, provider, and protector. As a priest, the father builds a bridge in order to access God. That bridge is also constructed for his family to reach God. As a provider, the father, like a hunter, leads the pack to the provisions needed for their survival. Finally, as a protector he encompasses priest and provider as a way of protection.

There were times when I watched my own courageous mother (Johnella) emulate the wisdom of Elimelech. She had to face grave options in moving to redeem her family. The famine of human relationships was introduced to me early in life when my mother and father separated and went their different ways. As early as I can remember, I watched my mother make hard choices. She had to work at both regular and odd jobs to make ends meet. Miraculously, the ends always met, and her choices, though not conventional by modern standards, proved she would not let her children starve.

My mother moved fourteen times within thirteen years. Like Elimelech and Naomi, we seemed destined to move from Bethlehem to Moab and then back again. To keep us all alive, Momma moved us around like we were nomads. The moves were interesting in the sense that I got a chance to meet many people and see many different things. It was only after I got older that I realized each move was just a few miles away from our starting point. But every move takes you further away from your comfort zone. Finally, you reach the beatific place of new beginnings.

My mother told me some years later that each move was to "get me closer to my goal of safety and security for my little ones." I do not know if she ever reached her goal, but it was intriguing to know that with every move she continued to serve her need to keep her family safe.

Not every move was advantageous. Like the move to an old house on Wayne Street. While we were living on Wayne Street, we received a telephone call one autumn Sunday morning at church to come home to our burning house. Everything we owned was lost in that fire. The fire burned all of our furniture and clothes—everything went up in smoke. The flames took our family mementos—the pictures of my great-grandmother (Mommo) and my grandmother (Grace) and my father (Daniel) were all gone in one fiery famine. We started out full. Each move cost my mother plenty, and yet we gained less. One truth I learned early from separation and death is that Ruth is no romance story; it is an exploration of reality.

Naomi in Moab, the Land of Tears (Ruth 1:2–5)

In a day when the life expectancy was twenty-seven, Naomi dealt three times with the brevity of life. My mother was widowed first on April 19, 1972. The telephone rang at approximately 4:00 a.m. I heard my mother answer the phone. A few moments later I heard her weep, and then there was silence. Without her uttering one word, I knew that something earth-shattering had happened. I dared not get up to see what had happened. I waited until my mother came into the room where my brother, Anthony, and I slept.

My mother sat on the edge of my bed and informed me that my father had succumbed to cardiac failure. He had died, she said, while visiting my older brother in Seattle, Washington. I asked my mother, "How are we going to make it now?" I was assuming even in estrangement that our resources were dependent on my father's existence. My mother's reply helped to shape a theology of provision for me at twelve years of age. Until that point, I had wrapped all of my security in a mother—my visible reality. I believed in God, and I thought His name was pronounced *Johnella*. But that morning I came to know God in a different way and that His name was pronounced *Jehovah-Jireh*. Momma said, "We are going to make it the way we always have; the Lord will provide for us." Those words have shaped my knowledge of what my real resources are as well as where they come from: "All things come of thee, and of thine own have we given thee" (1 Chron. 29:14 KJV).

Naomi's move led her from bread to famine and then to funerals. Three funerals and three graves Naomi would come to visit. Within a ten-year span she experienced the death of her husband and her two sons. A decade of tears is what the land of Moab offered her. Naomi's wealth, security, and provision were wrapped up in her husband. When Elimelech died Naomi's provision was contingent on her sons Mahlon and Kilion. Now that Naomi's sons were dead, she had lost all her resources. Or would this be the beginning of her learning who provided her real resources? Whether in Bethlehem or in Moab, God is the ultimate giver. "Every good and perfect gift is from above, coming down from the Father of the heavenly lights, who does not change like shifting shadows" (James 1:17).

What gifts did Elimelech, Mahlon, and Kilion leave for Orpah, Ruth, and Naomi? They left nothing but tears, grief, and bitterness. There were no grandchildren to brighten this scenario. Naomi was desolate. Sadly, she had no progeny—no one to pass the family bloodline on. Naomi felt that she had no one to turn to for consolation. At the end of the book, Ruth will know progeny and the joy of the word *pregnant*. The word *pregnant* means "full," and Naomi's life was empty. In the land of Moab, Naomi's life had been emptied of all of her previous joys.

Life is supposed to be filled with joy. The two words go together like a glove on a hand. But this is not always the case, is it? More times than any of us care to mention, life and bitterness or life and grief seem to be welded together. Life is often summed up for many in the words of the poet Paul Lawrence Dunbar:

> A crust of bread and a corner to sleep in,
> A minute to smile and an hour to weep in,
> A pint of joy and a peck of trouble,
> And never a laugh but the moans come double;
>> And that is life!
>>> —Paul Laurence Dunbar

A mother who has lost a child at the hands of a drunk driver or a father who has lost a child by suicide often live the rest of their lives with a dull desperation. The mother who is forced to face the decision of abortion lives her life always wondering what that child would have become. The couple who divorces lives in the aftermath of regret—did we do everything in our power to make this marriage work? We all know something about living without consolation.

I know people who have had to eat the stale bread of grief. This bread always leaves a bad taste of despair in their mouths. Specifically, I have known and wept with three grieving women: Gloria, whose daughter Mosha allegedly took her life by her own hand; Colin, whose daughter Britney was murdered on a Sunday afternoon in a shopping mall; and Marcile, whose husband Vernon's life was snuffed out while standing outside a convenience store a few blocks from home. Each of these persons I know personally, and I have watched them as they were forced to eat the bitter bread of grief.

We have the assurance of a God who loves us in such times of bereavement. We know the grief caused by the death of a loved one as well as the mercy that God gives to us during our times of loss. We can read of God's ability to get into our hurts with us while we suffer in Moab. God stoops down through Jesus Christ to scoop us up in His arms and caress us.

Such love toward us is seen in Jesus' benevolence toward a widow who lived in the town of Nain. Her only hope of fortune lay before her in a coffin. The mourners gathered in the streets displaying their grief for her loss. When Jesus saw this funeral procession and heard the wailing cries of the attendants, he was moved with love (see Luke 7:13). "Don't cry." That's easy for you to say, but you don't have any dead children. Little did this mother know that was exactly why Jesus was at the funeral. He had come to give life to those who were dead in trespasses and sin.

Jesus moved toward the coffin and touched it very gently. The pallbearers stopped. What happened next was more than what a grieving mother could ever be prepared to experience. Jesus said quietly yet authoritatively, "Young man, I say to you, get up!" The lungs of the young man filled with breath. His eyes opened, and he saw the black shrouds draped around the face and shoulders of the mourners. As he began to talk, he might have said, "I have seen wonderful things, and I have heard the voice of God." With this, Jesus graciously returned the boy to his mother. The people were correct in their confession: "God has come to help his people" (Luke 7:16). God has come to turn our mourning into dancing. That is precisely what God has come to do! This was God's way of pulling this widow mother from the land of bitterness into the land of blessedness.

One day a father named Jairus came to Jesus. He found himself in the land of Moab without leaving his hometown. Falling down on his knees in an undignified manner, he confessed his daughter was at home dying. Jairus asked Jesus to come and lay His hands on his daughter, believing if Jesus touched her she would be healed. Jesus honored his request. Jairus had no idea while on the way to his house that other people along the streets and in the crowd would need Jesus' healing assistance. Jesus was interrupted by a woman who had spent all of her resources trying to be healed. When all the medicines failed she reached out and touched the edge of the Divine Physician's robe. Jesus knew immediately that the power of healing had been drawn from Him. After the woman identified herself as the culprit, Jesus dismissed her with a brand new body. "Daughter, your faith has healed you. Go in peace and be freed from your suffering," He said (Mark 5:34). *If Jesus can do this for this sickly woman,* Jairus must have thought, *surely he can grant my daughter new life.*

Moab always comes at inopportune times. While Jesus was talking, a messenger delivered the news that no parent wants to hear, "Your daughter is dead. Why bother the teacher?" (Mark 5:35). What the messenger did not know is that Jesus specializes in things that seem impossible. Jesus is life, and He came to give life. He can do what no other power can do. Banishing fear from Jairus, Jesus continued on His rescue mission to Jairus's house. Accompanying Jesus was His "A Team" (Peter, James, and John). Upon entering the house, Jesus found the family and friends of Jairus wailing at the agony of death. There must have been shouts of how this could happen to such a promising girl. A cacophony of cries could be heard in and around the house.

"Everybody outside right now. Only the parents and my students may remain to witness this miracle," was Jesus' response to the mourners. Before the wet-eyed mother and father and the wide-eyed disciples Jesus took the little girl by the hand and said, "Get up." Miraculously the girl got up and started walking and playing. Jesus' orders were simple: Keep what you see a secret. Telling these eyewitnesses to keep the miracle quiet was the equivalent of giving them a megaphone. The first item on their to-do list was to tell as many people as possible what happened at Jairus's house. "Now give your daughter some bread to eat," said Jesus. Christ championed God's cause again by delivering His people from the land of Moab, the land of grief, to Bethlehem, the land of hope.

Crossing the Bar

Sunset and evening star,
And one clear call for me!
And may there be no moaning of the bar,
When I put out to sea.

For tho' from out our bourne of Time and Place
The flood may bear me far,
I hope to see my pilot face to face
When I have crossed the bar.

Lord Tennyson

Moab, Where the Lord's Hand Seems to Be Against You (Ruth 1:13)

Disappointment with God is a common theme among believers, but we rarely speak of it openly.

Disappointment is filled with the questions which, according to Phillip Yancey, we never ask out loud. Questions like, "If God is good, why is there so much evil in the world?" Or "If God is love why does He allow His children to experience unexplainable pain?" And "Why does God allow the innocent to suffer?" In his book *Why Bad Things Happen to Good People,* Rabbi Harold Kushner summarized disappointment with God when he spoke out loud for the many people who are disillusioned by suffering.

Who better than Naomi can answer our silent complaints about our disappointments with God? Her life is not a philosophical treatise about the problems of human suffering. On the other hand, Naomi teaches us that the God who delivers us from the bitterness of Moab is also able to show us how to start life over again. When Naomi arrived at the destination to decide where her life would lead her, she took into her counsel her daughters-in-law.

Even though they were from different backgrounds these three women shared common experiences. More than the marriages to Naomi's sons, Orpah and Ruth shared something deeper. The three women had a grave and a tombstone to remind them of how the joys of life can quickly turn into sorrows. Her daughters-in-law had the option of marrying again and starting over. But Naomi had come to the end of her child-bearing years and felt as if her life offered only bitterness and hopelessness.

Where are you in your pilgrimage with God? Do you feel that you have come full circle and have nothing to offer in life? Maybe you have expended all of your resources and feel as if God has a divine vendetta against you. Or, are you repeating Naomi's mantra that "it is far more bitter for me than it is for you." If you feel that way, you are a candidate for the sovereign God to do something special for you.

Remember, only those who have passed through the fire can lecture on asbestos. Naomi, Ruth, and Orpah were experts in the subject of asbestos—the inflammable material that ignites and burns away dregs of remorse. The Bible often uses fire to point out the trial that we go through. Paul says, "If any man builds on this foundation using gold, silver, costly stones, wood, hay or straw, his work will be shown for what it is, because the Day will bring it to light. It will be revealed with fire, and the fire will test the quality of each man's work. If what he has built survives, he will receive his reward. If it is burned up, he will suffer loss; he himself will be saved, but only as one escaping through the flames" (1 Cor. 3:12–15).

As the flames test the materials of your life, you have the opportunity to rebuild your broken world. We can only do this when we arise from a conviction that underlies the book of Ruth—that things do not happen by chance. God is sovereign, and everything is working in the cycle of His will.

Unfortunately Naomi concluded like many of us who have eaten the bitter bread of suffering. She believed that the hand of God was against her. The hand of God is often used in the Old Testament to reveal God's activity. The verb "gone out" often refers to the activities of armies going out with hostile intent. This seems to be the conclusion that Naomi reached about God's activities toward her. Naomi believed God had become hostile toward her.

Do you ever feel this way about the God who loves you? If so, chances are you need to start afresh with an understanding of who God is and how God acts. According to Naomi, the reason she could not encourage Orpah and Ruth to stay with her was because God was her enemy. Is this your bitter complaint against the God who loves you? If it is, now is the time to make an about-face and start your life over. Starting over is not difficult.

It is common among people to indict God when things go awry. Who is there better to blame than God? You do not have to go far without hearing an indictment against God. Attend a funeral of a high school senior killed in a car accident, and invariably someone will try to comfort the family with the words, "This is the will of the Lord." Often the burden of blame is placed on God because He is accused of being the great killjoy. Indictments toward God are often the syndrome that poisons the hearts of those who have been too long in Moab.

Are you stuck in Moab? Or maybe I should ask, "How long have you been in Moab, the place of bitterness and regret?" Remember, the longer you stay in Moab, the more embittered you will become. We are not created to stay in Moab but Bethlehem.

Mrs. Henry Dashwood in Jayne Austin's *Sense and Sensibility* found herself in Moab when her husband died. Lady Dashwood lost her fortune and was cast into poverty. She was a powerless widow with three daughters in the bleak world of Moab. Her husband's son John took over the residence in Norland after inheriting the estate, leaving Mrs. Henry Dashwood and her daughters feeling like aliens in their own home. Marriage was their only means of escape from the bitter, barren land of Moab. In order to break out of their bitterness, Mrs. Dashwood's daughters had to rely on their charm to secure husbands.

It is important to get out of Moab, to leave the land of weeping and head back to the House of Bread. But if we return to the land of granary only because we have learned that the famine is lifted, we are still attempting to live by bread alone. Our real need is to reconnect to the God who has graciously sustained us.

In the way that God emancipated Israel from the land of Egypt, He desires to deliver us from Moab. One way we can do this is through confession. "He who covers his sins will not prosper, but whoever confesses and forsakes them will have mercy" (Prov. 28:13 NKJV). The move to Moab was the result of a desperate choice, and unfortunately the entire family suffered for it. When we refuse to acknowledge our sins, it proves that we have not dealt honestly with them or judged them according to God's Word. True repentance involves the changing of our minds and moving in a new direction because of an inward conviction. It is moving from the bread of despair to the House of Bread. "The sacrifices of God are a broken spirit; a broken and a contrite heart, O God, you will not despise" (Ps. 51:17).

Confession is not just acknowledgment; it also involves announcement. First John 1:9 says, "If we confess our sins, he is faithful and just and will forgive us our sins and purify us from all unrighteousness" (say it publicly). You don't have to reveal the grimy details, but there should be open talk about getting out of Moab. Too often we want to relocate without telling anyone. There should be accountability in our change of address. Someone should be able to verify that we have moved out and moved on. In a marriage ceremony, the officiator asks if there are any witnesses. The reason for this is that it's difficult to undo the "I do" when others have heard you confess, "until death separates us."

One more truth regarding confession: it involves agreement. We covenant with God that Moab is not our first or final destination. If Moab is not reserved for us, why do we find ourselves in a God-forsaken place? Why are we engaged in activities displeasing to God and dissatisfying to ourselves? Naomi's loss teaches us that Moab can swallow the dreams of our present and rob us of our future. An interminable stay in Moab can make you insensitive to the voice of God. Maybe the hand of the Lord is not against us but rather it is for us. In order to get our attention His loving hand often disciplines our circumstances. "No discipline seems pleasant at the time, but painful. Later on, however, it produces a harvest of righteousness and peace for those who have been trained by it" (Heb. 12:11).

The reason why God permits these famines in the landscape of our lives is to remind us that He is our real bread. Leaving Bethlehem is always a tragic mistake, because there is nothing in Moab but distance, death, and dread. It is only when we can see the beauty of Bethlehem that we desire to go back home to it. Upon our return to Bethlehem, Moab becomes no more than a learnable inconvenience. Remember, Bethlehem is where God deals with the despair of Moab.

The House of Bread is the location of future promises fulfilled. The breadbaskets spill over and become abundance. The famine and the funerals are forgotten and replaced with festival. In Bethlehem the bitterness of the past gives way to the sweetness of the future. In Bethlehem the hope of the world is born—Jesus, the Bread of Life.

Chapter Two

How Do You Live When You Are Running on Empty?

RUTH 1:1–22

Imagine what happens when you're driving down a lonely highway and you "put the pedal to the metal" and the motor dies, or when you need to get somewhere but you're going nowhere. When you're looking for "vroom" but you're living on fumes? Is there anything more frightening than traveling unfamiliar roads without having enough fuel? If this is your experience, consider how Naomi and Ruth survived while running on empty.

The book of Ruth is really the tale of a woman named Naomi whose journey down the road of life is stalled in a desolate desert. Hurt has punctured Naomi's fuel tank. Grief has killed her passion for life. Living is as pointless to her as dreaming. The vicious world has left her stranded with no raison d'etre—no will to live. But she is not alone—not by a long shot! Naomi is traveling with a passenger in her stranded life—a lonely young woman named Ruth. So Naomi, stranded and desperate turns to Ruth and says:

> Do not call me Naomi; call me Mara,
> for the Almighty has dealt very bitterly
> with me. I went out full, and the LORD has
> brought me home again empty. Why do you
> call me Naomi, since the LORD has testified
> against me, and the Almighty has afflicted
> me? (Ruth 1:20–21 NKJV)

Conversely, Ruth turns to her and says, "Listen Naomi, life has not been all that good to me either, but I beg you, 'don't urge me to leave you or to turn back from you. Where you go I will go, and where you stay I will stay. Your people will be my people and your God my God.'"

So Naomi returns from the country of Moab along with Ruth, the Moabitess, her daughter-in-law. At last, wearied from their long journey, they come to Bethlehem at the beginning of the barley harvest. Naomi's despair is etching her soul with the acid of bitterness.

Is Naomi's case utterly strange to you? Have you never been to the place where you also had to say, "I went out full and the Lord has brought me home again empty"? So we must ask, What do you do when you are running on empty? How do you make it when you are depleted and you have not one ounce of stamina to move the tonnage of this world's cares? Let us start this story over at the beginning.

Once upon a time in the town of Bethlehem there lived a family of Jewish descent. They lived in the troubled, chaotic years between the times of the Judges and the crowning of King Saul. This family made their living from the hard work of an artist's hands, fashioning glorious art from dead clay. The artist's name was Elimelech. He was a good potter, and he made a good living for his family. This simple artist lived well, eating wheat from the fertile land and drinking wine from the lush vineyards of Bethlehem. Elimelech and his family were the beneficiaries of their hard-working ancestors. They drank from wells they never dug and ate bread from the harvest conferred by the generous sun and rain of the Lord God Himself. Elimelech provided well for his family. Had they been anything but Jewish, they might have said they lived "high on the hog."

But Bethlehem's idyllic living did not last long. Suddenly the land was blasted by scorching winds and famines. No rain fell upon the earth. Finally, by the year's end, all of the grain fields had been scorched by the angry sun. This family of Bethlehem found themselves caught between starvation and death. They asked, "What are we to do?" There was no grain to be bought. Further, their living dried up like the sun-parched fields because nobody buys pottery in hard times. Starving artists really starve in times like these! You cannot eat porridge from a dust bowl.

But what kind of man was this artist Elimelech?

In a patriarchal world, the father was the dominant figure. He ran the show, especially when the show was poor. So he said to Naomi, his wife, "Let's leave for the east."

"But that is Arabia," she said.

"Better to live in Arabia than to die in Israel. We will go to Moab, and maybe there we can start over. We will eat again and put some certainty back in our lives."

And so they did. It seemed a wise move. Wisdom measures the days. A wise person is one who knows what time it is in life.

The opening lines of the story of Ruth present us with a person of courage. Elimelech was a survivor. He had the courage to change lanes in life. He seemed willing to head in another direction, knowing God can meet us anywhere we invite his presence to come. He said to his wife and sons, "Let's move eastward to Moab. Maybe things will work out for us there."

The Hebrew names of the people in this story bring insight into what takes place. Elimelech's name means "my God is king." Bethlehem means "house of bread." But there now is no barley in the "house of bread." Exit the idyllic story. Down with the happy ending!

The journey begins. They walk from Bethlehem eastward to Moab. Glory reigns! There is bread, life, hope. The artist finds a source of clay. His wheel spins again with his astounding art. Elimelech succeeds. His pottery becomes the choice art of Arabia. It is better than good; it's fantastic.

Suddenly Elimelech dies and his death strikes at the heart of Naomi. Barren emptiness starves her hope. She wails, "Not only is there barrenness in Bethlehem and death and dirt in my house; I am left now in a wasteland of existence. My resources have been taken away from me." How cruel is life? Just as the bluebird of happiness begins singing outside her gallery, night comes. On the edge of her hope falls the dark crepe of death. But it's amazing how resilient life is, even in the face of death. In the words of T. S. Eliot's *Love Song of J. Alfred Prufrock,* we measure our lives out in coffee spoons. Life is bleak. Life is tough! But you, like Naomi, have a passenger in your journey to the future. This passenger knows you are running on empty. It is the transforming Spirit of God, the Holy Spirit, the Spirit of hope. The Spirit of God forces you to get back at it, to refuel for the road and stay on the journey.

The fuel level was running low in the tank of Jesus' disciples. As they trembled beneath the prediction of Jesus' death, He assured His friends that He would not leave them as orphans. Aware of their running on empty, He refueled them with words of comfort. "Do not let your hearts be troubled. Trust in God; trust also in me. . . . if I go and prepare a place for you, I will come back and take you to be with me that you also may be where I am" (John 14:1, 3). Although His disciples were refueled there was no sustaining presence to keep them energized if Jesus was going away. Therefore, questions concerning His whereabouts were on the lips of His disciples. Even with the road map detailing His location, there was no guarantee there would be enough fuel to complete the journey.

To breathe life into the disciples' troubled hearts, Jesus left them a gift—the Holy Spirit. He would transform them from fear to faith. Until now Jesus had been their comforter, but now He would give them the Spirit of hope: "And I will ask the Father, and he will give you another Counselor to be with you forever—the Spirit of truth. The world cannot accept him, because it neither sees him nor knows him. But you know him, for he lives with you and will be in you" (John 14:16–17).

The Spirit is called to assist you when you are running on empty. Emptiness can be defined in many ways. The world is full of walking illustrations of empty living. They hug the street corners of big cities. The people who suffer from anorexic and bulimic living are fed up with emptiness. Here is where the Spirit invades all spaces and replaces it with His presence. "Do not get drunk on wine, which leads to debauchery. Instead, be filled with the Spirit" (Eph. 5:18).

Life had dealt Naomi not just a blow but a knockout! She staggered to her knees, but she was not yet down. In the middle of conflict and catastrophe, Naomi pulled herself up and moved forward. She was steady with her decisions. She decided to remain in Moab. Her sons, Mahlon and Kilion, had reached the age of marriage, and so she said to them, "Find yourselves wives." They did . . . among the Moabites. The name of one of her sons means "Weakness" (Mahlon). The name of the other means "Sickness" (Kilion). Imagine those names on your marriage invitations. Still Naomi had hope.

"Weakness" and "Sickness" marry Orpah and Ruth. Things go well for a while. Nothing out of the ordinary happens. Two Jewish boys, Hebrews, marry two Arab women. Here is a lesson in race relations to be studied carefully. Arabs and Jews are the racial wars of every era. Life is to be measured by nouns, not adjectives. But to look at people by nouns, black and white are in some ways the most unworthy of adjectives.

Carlyle Marney said, "One of the great adventures of life for every human being is to learn to put adjectives and nouns in their proper places." Tall and short may be adjectives that describe the shape and size of a person, but they tell us nothing about the personhood of the person. They merely describe. "A creation of God" would be a better way, would it not, to describe the personhood of every human being.

Those of us who have lived in the South and have been reared in southern towns and cities know of a time where there was a group of people who were identified not by their personhood but by their adjectives. They were called Negroes. This adjective often was elevated to the place of noun. So when people met a person, they did not meet a person; they met a color—they met a race. But Naomi taught her boys, "Seek a wife. Remember, nouns are what matter, not adjectives. Do not go looking for a particular color of person; look for a real person." And so they did; her sons looked beyond the adjectives and found real persons to marry.

Unfortunately, the demons of barrenness were not ready to leave this family. Emptiness has a way of stalking those it has made to suffer. The emptiness of the barley fields in Bethlehem, the death of

Elimelech, and now a further emptiness devoured their souls from the center. The sons of Naomi—Sickness and Weakness—died, and three widows were left—Naomi, Orpah, and Ruth. Remember, the wise person knows what time it is in life. Naomi was able to read the times, and she realized now Moab stalked her peace with weightiness. Moab was heavy with bereaved memories—the loss of a husband, the death of her sons, and the widowing of her daughters-in-law.

As Naomi considered the time, she began to wonder, *What will I do now—now that all joy has been taken away from me?* She began to focus on herself. There were rumors on the whispered wind. The caravan drivers who came through Moab dropped the word: after ten years of famine in Bethlehem it was once again the land of plenty. There had been a lifting of the desert sanctions. The absence of barley had given way to the presence of grain. Bethlehem had once again earned its name—the house of bread was indeed the house of bread.

Naomi concluded that Moab was a dead land, empty as the desolation of her heart. *There is no reason for me to remain,* she told herself. *My husband and my sons are gone. Their headstones jut into the sands of Arabia. I am heading west to the house of bread. I have family and relatives there; maybe they will take pity on my emptiness.* Naomi pulled out her luggage and began folding her garments into it. She filled her cases with the tiny remnants of all that was left of the pottery of Elimelech. She gathered her goods and said good-bye to Orpah and Ruth.

And as the custom was, both Orpah and Ruth began walking westward toward Bethlehem with their mother-in-law. They were a heartbroken trio of widows—ashen of complexion. They were as silent as the grave. Finally, Naomi said to her daughters, "I am going now." They protested, "We want to go with you."

"No, that is not a good thing," Naomi replied. "What do you want me to do? There are no more sons in my womb, and even if there were, would you wait twenty years for them to be grown so you could marry them?" Orpah quickly complied, "You are right. I will leave you now." And so with the small remnants of her short marriage, Orpah headed back to Moab.

The biblical storyteller unravels this word *return* for us. Yet, the only person who really could return to Bethlehem was Naomi. Ruth and Orpah had never lived there, so technically they never left it. Naomi became forceful, "Go back to your mother's house!" Orpah went! Ruth remained! What is the point of Ruth's stick-to-it-iveness—her sweet allegiance? What is it that causes her to cling to her mother-in-law? Mothers-in-law and daughters-in-law are not usually studies in allegiance. They are more often antagonists. But here is the rewriting of life's story: Ruth actually submits herself to become the authentic daughter whom Naomi has never had.

Naomi said, "Ruth"—and here again a play on names comes up again—Naomi's name means "peaceful." Ruth means "refresher." And at that very moment when Naomi has become bone dry, bitter, and at the end of her wits, she begins getting refreshment from Ruth, who says, "I . . . I can't leave you."

Naomi says, "Oh yes you can."

"No, I can't leave you."

Naomi becomes insistent, "Leave and go back to your mother's house."

Ruth replies with these immortal words— "Entreat me not to leave you" (Ruth 1:16 NKJV). These words are not to be read casually. These are pledges. This is a vow that Ruth made: "Entreat me not to leave you." Ruth became a beggar, begging for fullness from an empty woman. "Naomi, I beg you, do not make me go back home. I want to stay where you are, peacefulness. I have learned peace at the hem of your dress. I beg you, do not make me go back home. 'Entreat me not to leave you, or to turn back from following after you; for wherever you go, I will go; and wherever you lodge, I will lodge; your people shall be my people, and your God, my God. Where you die, I will die, and there will I be buried. The LORD do so to me, and more also, if anything but death parts you and me'" (Ruth 1:16–17 NKJV).

When Ruth spoke those words Naomi's eyes were tightened by stinging fire. Tears burned down her dry cheeks, and she looked back into the face of a girl, a Moabite. What called forth her joy? It was the phrase "your God shall be my God." She was able to say it because Naomi had never seen her as a racial adjective, but had treated her as a whole noun. Here, she had never called her my son's Moabite wife, but just plain Ruth. And when Ruth recognized the dignity and the value, the self-worth and esteem that Naomi had given her, she had peace. They drank the cup of life together! They understood they were partners in the barren journey. She saw that there was confusion in Naomi. Ruth said to her, "I want to give you my refreshment, because that's what true spiritual partnership does. You have given me peace; my gift to you is refreshment."

The exchange between Naomi and Ruth reveals something about the benefits of giving. These gifts are not to be confused with perishable commodities. These are gems from the heart. Peace and refreshment—two pearls of great price. You need the gift of peace in order to cope with the uncertainties of the future. On the other hand, you need the gift of refreshment to quench the realities of a bitter past. "A generous man will prosper; he who refreshes others will himself be refreshed" (Prov. 11:25). Life is never sweeter than when we give the essence of ourselves away to someone else. Jesus gave the essence of Himself away to His disciples when He said, "Peace I leave with you; my peace I give you. I do not give to you as the world gives. Do not let your hearts be troubled and do not be afraid" (John 14:27).

"Your God shall be my God." These words are the heart of God's love. Ruth was a Gentile who had learned the love of God from a suffering servant. "Your God shall be my God." This was a Moabite proselyte saying, "I am a woman who has worshiped at the shrine of pagan idolatry." Not once had Naomi chastised her for the way she worshiped. Naomi just accepted her on the terms of who she was. She was Ruth, a refreshing spring in a dry, barren place. And now she had added glory to Naomi's plain, dead faith. She confessed, "Your God shall be my God; your ways, God's values, God's truths, God's teachings, God's way of life. All that Yahweh means to Israel is what I want Yahweh to mean to me. Racially we may be different, but those differences are little adjectives, and we serve the God of nouns. It will not take long for me to learn the way of your kin. If your family is anything like you, they will be my family too. Your God shall be my God."

Why should we be amazed that God would pick such a woman to be the great grandmother of Jesus? This is a key word if we would understand the story of the redeemer. "Redeemer" . . . now there's a significant noun! Jesus understood this noun. "Come follow me," said Jesus, "—lay aside the tiny adjectives that describe you. I am a God of nouns." "Come follow me," Jesus said to Matthew. How dare Jesus call a tax collector to be a disciple! But notice that Jesus did not call him a "Jewish" tax collector. "Jewish" is an adjective. Jesus said, "I am not into adjectives."

"Come follow me, Simon the Zealot." A zealot named Simon came. And the people said, "How could he get a religious insurrectionist to work on behalf of kingdom building?" Jesus said, "You call him rebellious—I call him Simon. Just the nouns, if you please. You can have your adjectives!"

That is the beauty of what God does for us. He never calls, "Come here, you drunken bum. Come here, you slinky harlot! Come here, you devious prostitute. Come here, you man-loving gay." Jesus never called anyone by such adjectives. He just said, "John, come to me. Frankie, come to me." And all the adjectives that the world has forced you to wear, you can drop. Once I call you unto Myself . . . I am out to change the horrible adjectives that others have used to describe your life. You have been redeemed and placed as a good, solid, unqualified noun in the lexicon of God. *Your God shall be my God.*

Paul wrote a letter to the church in Galatia. The theme of his message was freedom. Grace transcends the law, he said. When I called you, you were neither Jew nor Gentile. You were neither bond nor free, male nor female. We are one in Christ Jesus (Gal. 3:28). This is where Christ has come to do his work, to change the descriptions of our lives, for God to be our God. *Your God shall be my God.* Your people shall be my people. Where you live, I will live. Where you go, I will go. And let there be nothing but death that separates us. Even then we will be buried in the same cemetery.

Tears dropped from the face of Naomi as she looked at this unfailing partner in life. She was verbally and emotionally clinging to her, and she cried, "Let's walk together then. My God will be your God."

Remember the myth of Prometheus? Zeus had given a commandment that God would not have anything to do with humanity. When Zeus turned his back, Prometheus saw a man stumbling in the dark and shivering in the cold and took compassion on him. Prometheus stole fire from the comfortable gods and went down to earth to give the fire to them in darkness, to bring warmth to the frigid earth. When Zeus discovered that Prometheus had stolen fire, he exiled Prometheus from Olympus and chained him to a rock. To punish Prometheus, Zeus sent vultures at daybreak and ripped his liver out each morning. It grew back during the day. Life is full of pain; it is an endless hell of suffering. Naomi, like Prometheus, knew the horror of constant emptiness and pain.

So these wounded widows walked! Westward they walked! Ever westward Naomi and Ruth journeyed. After weeks of walking, Naomi finally made her way to the threshold of Bethlehem. The word quickly circulated throughout the house of bread that Emilelech's widow was back. Naomi was home at last. Sister Peace had come back to Bethlehem. And people cheered and applauded and celebrated that peace once more had come back to the house of bread. But in spite of Ruth's loyalty, Naomi had become a cynic—an embittered woman. Naomi said, "Do not call me Naomi. God has dealt bitterly with me. Call me Mara because I have suffered afflictions from the hand of God."

Naomi spoke a lot like us in what I call egotistic defiance. Cynicism is an egocentric way of looking at life when life does not turn out like we planned it. It is as though we have done something wrong and are sentenced to inherit this affliction that has come into our lives. I do not mean to burst your egomaniacal disposition, but you are not so important in the cosmos that God would postpone all his management of the vast universe just to execute affliction on you for the fun of watching you suffer.

The creation narrative is so vital to the understanding of redemption that Simon Wiesenthal, the Holocaust survivor, says, "In creation, God desisted from being everything so you could be something." In the vernacular of a card game, God gave away some of His power to you so you could find significance in God's universe.

Therefore, if God could so humble Himself, why can we not do it? We are neither so important nor are the decisions we make so cosmic that whatever we do will postpone the sunrise or let God make us inherit all the inflictions of life. It is more likely that some afflictions have come your way so God can draw from you the best out of your life.

Naomi virtually wags her finger in the face of your cynicism. Hear her speak to the burden you carry—the weight of guilt and shame you will not lay aside. Give up your self-absorbed idea that the reason you did not get the job you wanted was because of sin in your life. Quit saying the reason you had trouble was because you were involved in odd activities. God is not playing the game of "I'll get you back." God is not a God who enjoys sweet revenge. Nor does God say, "You do right and I'll bless you. Do wrong and I'll curse you." We would not survive a day if God should abandon grace and take on that attitude.

"Do not call me Naomi," cried the bitter widow. "Call me bitterness, for God has afflicted me. I am dealing with affliction." And so she said, "When I came to Bethlehem, I was full. I had Elimelech, my husband, my friend, my confidante. I had Mahlon and I had Kilion, my children. I was full when I went out, but now I have come back empty, having buried all of them in a foreign land. Do not call me peaceful. I have no peace. I own nothing but my despair. I have many wounds. I have burdens. I have stripes. The Almighty has dealt bitterly with me."

God is a God who loves the broken. He adores the crushed of spirit. God can help you when you go out full and come back empty. God knows that life has a way of emptying you. Life has a way of draining your joy, your hopes, your dreams, your power, your position, your love. So how do we make it when we are on empty? One thing you can do is learn how to cling to hope in the face of despair. Never underestimate the power of hope. Hope becomes a choice, a choice in which you stare life in the face and say, "I am going to make it. I may have to play in a symphony with only one string on my violin, but I am determined to live. I will make music."

During a freshman humanities course the class had to interpret the painting of Watts. It was his famous portrait of a woman sitting on top of the world. She had one breast exposed and was nursing her baby. Her brow was bandaged, dirty, and bloody, and her dress was tattered and torn. She had one sandal on and one off. She appeared defeated, but there she was sitting on top of the world! Watts was trying to get the observer to see this as a portrait of hope. It may not look like hope when your head is bandaged, your breast is exposed, and your clothes are torn, but I have learned this is how hope often appears. If there is any piece of survival left, I can make it. I do not have to own a whole loaf of bread; I just need a piece. Neither do I have to have a full cup of water—just a thimbleful will do.

> Whether we be young or old,
> Our destiny, our being's heart and home,
> Is with infinitude, and only there;
> With hope it is, hope that can never die,
> Effort, and expectation, and desire,
> And something evermove about to be
> —William Wordsworth, *The Prelude,* bk. 4,
> lines 603–608

Hope.

To go out full and come back empty, to practice your hope in the face of despair, is to learn the art of making the best out of a mess. It is the fine art of making lemonade out of lemons. Squeeze a little lemon in a little water, add some sugar, and presto—lemonade! Remember, if you can't make lemonade, make sugar water. God used Ruth to teach this simple recipe to Naomi. Ruth had said to her mother-in-law, "I'm not going to call you Bitter, but Sweetie." Today, you can lift up your soul and say, "I came in bitter, but I've got a new name. Call me Sweetie. God has given me delight in my life."

When you go out empty and you come in, return to where your hope and your help can be found. No matter the lemons, the recipe is real!

The church is a blessed privilege in the life of Christians. Primarily the church is a filling station. Enter the church empty and find yourself full. The filling is not an isolated experience. As the worshipers stand in reverence for the reading of the Scripture, others are clapping their hands in appreciation to God. Some are singing hymns and spiritual songs, while others are consenting to the preaching of God's Word. In the midst of these worship activities, the Spirit reminds us, "I have not forgotten you. I know your name. I know your address." The next time you go out full and come back empty, just remember God is able to keep all His promises. He is the source of fueling when you are running on empty.

I was invited to preach for the Southern Baptists in Palestine, Texas. Taking the trip with me was a friend. We hadn't been traveling very long when it started raining, and the windshield wipers of my car got tangled up. I somehow knew it was going to be a challenging day. I remember thinking, *I hope my sermon does not end up as crossed as these wipers.* Suddenly the fuel level indicator flashed on.

I felt absolutely alone. I was running on empty. I began looking for a service station. There was none in sight, not a sign indicating one was near.

Thankfully, I had a fancy little car equipped with a range indicator button to find out how many miles I had left to run before I was completely out of gas. There it was, light on, depressing the button, ten miles flashed up. I said, *I can make it. I am sure I can find a service station in the next ten miles.*

Consequently, like Naomi, my despair was not total—I had a passenger with me in the car. I said to my traveling companion, David Boyle, "All right, Boyle, you and I are going to be pushing this car if we don't find a station." Then, suddenly the fuel gauge didn't indicate anything. It just started flashing hyphens across the LCD, a computer-driven dash. Panic gripped me. Despair and desperation were rising. Suddenly I remembered I had the car's manual in my glove compartment. I said, "Boyle, open the glove compartment. Flip through the pages of that manual and find out the details about the fuel gauge."

Boyle opened the manual and started reading. "When the dash light moves past "E" and flashes hyphens, do not panic. Once you get to this level, there is a built-in reserve tank that will kick in and give you an extra thirty miles."

We not only have a fellow passenger, we have a manual. God has given us the fellow passenger of His Spirit, and God has given us the manual of His mind. When you find yourself empty, pick up the manual, read the instructions, and let God take over from there. Remember, the God who brings you out is the same God who can take you in.

No sensible traveler takes a journey without directions. Abraham journeyed, not knowing where he was going to end up. Yet, he knew the direction of his pilgrimage was westward. If we are going to have a good journey we also need navigation. Modern technology provides some cars with built-in navigational systems. The purpose of this navigational program is to facilitate the driver with accuracy. For instance, you program the address of your destination, and step by step the navigational program talks you through every detail. The responsibility is on the driver to trust the computer to supervise the process. I must confess I don't always listen to the navigational instructions. But each time I violate the voice command, I prolong the trip.

Likewise, the Bible is our road map. It knows the heart and intent of every person. To read the Scripture is to hear God's voice. To obey God's command demonstrates you love Him. To disrespect God's voice in Scripture prolongs your journey. Other times it can make your journey through life difficult. You will run into dead-ends. Also, you will miss your exit or travel in the wrong direction. To obey the Word of God brings life in its fullness.

The words of the hymn "Guide Me, O Thou Great Jehovah" speak to this truth. "Guide me, O thou great Jehovah, pilgrim through this barren land. I am weak, but Thou art mighty. Hold me with Thy powerful hand. Bread of heaven, feed me 'til I want no more" *(The African American Heritage Hymnal,* No. 138.)

This is one reason we come to church. This is the community of faith. The church is the house of bread. Here we surrender our bitterness to enjoy the sweetness of God. We come because there is bread here. We come to the assembly because there is a filling. Thank you, Lord, for filling us 'til we want no more.

Chapter Three

The High Art of Grubbing for Grace

RUTH 2:1–7

The world contains two definite types of people: the rich who continually believe themselves poor and struggle to be richer and the poor who feel themselves rich but have not a pittance to prove their wealth.

Ruth was a person who never stopped to bewail her poverty. It is not altogether clear whether Ruth was aware of their destitution. The sun was shining in Bethlehem. Ruth had her wonderful mother-in-law with her. There was free grain on the earth in

Bethlehem—just lying there—just waiting to be picked up, threshed, ground into meal, and baked for breakfast.

The words *miser* and *miserable* have the same origin. One is a noun; the other is an adjective. Both words describe the person who becomes a hoarder. As words they are not impertinent until you put a face on them. Ruth must have asked why anyone with the option to be happy would settle for misery.

Ruth would never have understood "Hetty" Green, who is remembered as America's greatest miser. Hetty died in 1916 and left an estate valued at 100 million dollars. Her diet consisted of cold oatmeal to avoid the cost of heating it. Her son suffered a leg amputation because she delayed his medical assistance while she was looking for a free clinic. His leg was so infected that it became incurable.

The house she lived in was a run-down shack. It was an eyesore to the people in the neighborhood. She wore the same old clothes regardless of the weather. Sometimes she pushed an old cart and collected trash. When Hetty died, it was discovered that she had the financial means to have lived like a queen.

Why would anyone with the money to live like royalty choose to live like a miser? Could the answer be that Hetty was eccentric? Or was she insane? Maybe she was both, but no one could validate either claim. Hetty's disposition as a miser knew no limits. She hastened her own death by bringing on an attack of apoplexy while arguing about the value of drinking skimmed milk! Hetty is an analogy of too many Christians with unlimited resources within their reach; yet, they settle for a parsimonious existence.

This was not Ruth's plight. She would not sink into a life of bitterness. Ruth had had her fill of grief in the land of Moab. The graves of her husband, brother-in-law, and father-in-law were in her past. She was positioning herself for a grand future. The future was unknown to Ruth but not to Naomi's God. And now Naomi had come to the land of bread, and she wanted her loaf. All others in the "house of bread" might settle for less than what was available to them, but not Ruth.

Will You Let Me Go and Glean?

The fresh stalks of barley were ripe and ready for harvesting. The fields were populated with reapers. The sacks of the gleaners were spilling over with wheat. The smell of life was in the air. The smell of barley was a refreshing difference for the two women. The only fragrance they had worn was the ointment of the dead. The aroma of bread was a welcomed difference from the smell of death left behind in Moab.

The smell of harvest was an invitation for the women to go out into the field. Ruth could no longer restrain herself from the field of plenty. Why starve when there was plenty of bread to spare? *Besides,* she thought, *we have starved long enough in matters beyond our control. Now we are present in this land of beauty, bounty, and blessing.* "Let me go to the fields and pick up the leftover grain behind anyone in whose eyes I find favor" (Ruth 2:2).

Ruth was unaware of the providential ways of Naomi's God. She was a resident alien in Bethlehem and had not been tutored in the subject of grace. Jehovah had already provided for Ruth without her knowing or asking. Gleaning was not dependent on the whim of the landowners. It was a right specifically included in the law for widows: "When you are harvesting in your field and you overlook a sheaf, do not go back to get it. Leave it for the alien, the fatherless and the widow, so that the LORD your God may bless you in all the work of your hands" (Deut. 24:19).

Ruth didn't know it, but God was orchestrating each move toward His purpose. A cursory reading of Ruth's story may keep the necessity of faith hidden from you. At the heart of this narrative Ruth is a person of faith. Although Yahweh was a new experience for her, Ruth was a quick learner. Nothing of significance happened in Bethlehem or with Ruth that is not attached to faith. Ruth was acting on pure faith. She was preparing to enter territory unfamiliar to her as an alien or foreigner in Bethlehem. Moreover, Ruth was to trust in God to protect her in hostile fields and to provide for her where the harvest fields looked scarce.

Ruth found favor in the only eyes that mattered—Jehovah. Bethlehem was God's special land; it was in Bethlehem that Ruth and Naomi would start over. Why? Because the bitterness of Moab was in the widows' past, and it was time to start over. Moab was only fifty miles away from the neighboring land of Bethlehem. The Moabites were the descendants of Lot from an incestuous union with his firstborn daughter. Moabites were the Jews' enemies because of the way they treated Israel during their journey from Egypt to Canaan. During the time of the judges, the Moabites invaded Israel and ruled over them for eighteen years. They were an arrogant people whom God disdained. The Lord declared, "Moab is My wash basin" (Ps. 60:8 NKJV) —a picture of a humiliated nation washing the feet of the conquering soldiers.

At that time, all of Moab's hostility was behind Ruth and Naomi. Today was a new day and a time to start over. Maybe your past is casting an elongated shadow over your present as well as your future. It seems you can't escape from past disappointments. You have tried to relocate from one city to the rustic living of a quiet town. Probably you have attempted to forget and move forward, only to be reminded of what you have left behind. If this describes your situation, let me recommend that starting over has little to do with geographical relocation. New beginnings have everything to do with a reorientation of attitude.

After the resurrection the disciples of Jesus needed a fresh start. One of Jesus' primary students, Peter the Rock, was discouraged. Peter felt his only alternative for facing the future was to return to his previous way of life. Not knowing what to do next, Peter said, "I'm going fishing" (see John 21:3). Peter was unaware of the possibilities awaiting him. He was also ignorant of what was coming next in his life with Jesus alive. He would never know future hope if he continued to distance himself from Jesus. But with Jesus alive the future was full of opportunities after Pentecost. In the early morning Jesus extended to Peter a foundation on which to stand.

Peter had acted more like a pebble than a rock. During Pentecost we see a new vitality breathed into the empty lungs of Simon Peter. Previously, Peter vacillated as a Christ follower. The evidence of Peter starting over is witnessed as he preached the Pentecost sermon. Imbued with the Holy Spirit, Peter reported to his hearers that they could also start over: "Repent and be baptized, every one of you, in the name of Jesus Christ for the forgiveness of your sins. And you will receive the gift of the Holy Spirit" (Acts 2:38). How could a person like Peter pronounce with confidence that we can start over? Because starting over is also Peter's story.

By the way, there is nothing embarrassing about starting over. Each day is a gift to begin again. "Because of the LORD's great love we are not consumed, for his compassions never fail. They are new every morning; great is your faithfulness" (Lam. 3:22–23).

Ruth understood that when God is in charge, you can always start over by coming back to God. He is the grand reply to failure. The Gracious One is where genuine starting over begins. The first step in starting over is to admit your need for God. If you do not think you have a need for God, this would be the best of all times for you to pause and reflect on all the seasons of your life in which you have abandoned the promises of God. Life begins in the grand U-turn, where you spin the vehicle of self-interest and head directly for obedience. Relinquish the past. Start moving in a new direction that is mapped out just for you. Then sit back and enjoy the grace of new life.

Aptitude is a necessary quality for seasoned and inexperienced drivers alike. The ability to talk on a cell phone, pay attention to the road, listen to music, and navigate through heavy traffic takes the driving skills of an A. J. Foyt. During Christmas of 2001, my son, Ralph Jr., was home for the holidays.

One Friday Ralph had been out most of the day with his brother, Ralpheal, and Jamal, his road buddies. As the night matured toward early morning I placed a call to check on his location. Ralph replied, "I'm on Beltway 8 on my way home."

After thirty minutes passed, I called again, concerned because Ralph was an inexperienced driver. Again, I asked about his location. Only this time Ralph's reply was less cordial. But he assured me he would be home in approximately thirty minutes. I returned no hostile verbal fire toward my son. I knew Ralph needed to make directional errors in order to find his way through the labyrinth of Houston. On the other hand, as a father I was concerned since I knew about the jungle mentality of the big city. After another thirty minutes passed, I decided to call Ralph again. Only this time I would inquire specifically about his location on the Beltway.

When Ralph answered the phone, his disapproval of my incessant calling was evident. His irritation was not a concern for me at the twilight hour in Houston. "Where are you, Ralph?" I asked.

"On the Beltway," he answered.

"Where on the Beltway?"

"I'm approaching South Post Oak," he replied.

"In what direction are you traveling?"

"South," he said, exasperated.

Then I said, "Ralph, you are traveling in the wrong direction. Exit and get back on the Beltway and travel north. You will pass Highway 59. Keep north. Next you will come to Interstate 10. Keep north on the Beltway. When you see Highway 290 the scenery ought to look familiar, but remember to keep north until you see the north Dallas elevator. You can handle it from there."

Ralph assured me he could handle the drive with the new directions. As a father I trusted Ralph to stay with the charted course. But follow-up is a good preventive measure. Because of my concern for my son, I decided to get in the car and go meet him.

Therefore, I pulled over and waited at Highway 45 and Airtex for Ralph to go through the toll booth, get on Highway 45, and follow him home. Intuitively, I felt the need to call Ralph once more. This time Ralph answered warmly because the landscape of Houston was becoming familiar to him. But what he said next was cause for alarm. "Daddy, I'm going in the right direction, but I don't have money to pay the final toll. Neither do I have enough gas to get home."

I said, "Ralph, stay north and before you get to the toll booth get on the shoulder lane and wait for me. I'll have my hazard lights on. When I spot you I'll flash my lights." I saw the green Land Cruiser on the shoulder of the Beltway. I pulled to the side of Ralph and blew the horn. Ralph followed me to the toll booth. When I passed through the toll, Ralph stopped. In my rearview mirror I saw Ralph explaining to the attendant that he was penniless. As Ralph pleaded his case, I noticed the attendant waving Ralph through, as he continued his dissertation on destitution. Finally, the attendant notified Ralph that his father had already paid his toll.

After reaching the service station I swiped my Shell gasoline card and had Ralph pull forward and fill his empty gas tank. Ralph had enough petroleum to take his brother and cousin home. Ralph pulled out and started over after a long night of frustration, irritation, and misdirection. And so can you when you realize your fare has been paid at Calvary and the Holy Spirit has retooled you for life's journey.

To do anything else is to go on living the dying life. But why continue such a life? Why continue to glut yourself on the bread that can't fill? Why drink from the streams that can never slake your thirst? When the quality of hope is gone, what is there to live for? Sadly, many people are grubbing through life like the gleaners in the barley fields. They scratch at the dry ground of life when the gifts of life are only a U-turn away.

To glean in the fields is not a fashionable art. When you glean in the field, you chafe the hands. You dig in the arid earth until your fingernails bleed, and you do it because it is a way to live. But it is not a life of ease or dignity. You bend until your back breaks and your knees are scarred. Consequently, life does not always come easy. Ruth did not glean as a person of elitist standing, but in order to provide food for herself and Naomi. You go to the field hard or not, because you want to make life endurable. Regardless of the pain of working, you toughen up and dig in because you have a family to feed.

Behind the Harvesters

"So [Ruth] went out and began to glean in the fields behind the harvesters" (see Ruth 2:3). There is a glorious happenstance in those events. On earth, they look like coincidence, but they require the architecture of angels. No happenstance here. God was in charge, and He was stirring up a shower of grace to dump on the gleaners of Bethlehem. As it turned out, Ruth found herself working in a field belonging to Boaz, who was from the clan of Elimelech, her lately deceased father-in-law!

Ruth began a new phase in her life. Ruth was a gleaner! Ruth did not understand the glory God had hidden in her new job. But Ruth would soon find it was filled with significance. Ruth was working in the field beside the nameless poor of Bethlehem. Gleaners need no formal introduction. Poverty makes them brothers and sisters and leaves them without names. Ruth had no idea she was gleaning the leftovers in the barley field of an owner unknown to her. Ruth didn't know she was working outside the protection of Naomi's hut and was not ignorant to the dangers surrounding her.

Ruth initially believed she came to this particular field by chance to work. This story points to the truth that men do not control events, but the hand of God is working His purpose out. The purposes of God are great. But many people believe starting over means starting without difficulty. Often new beginnings are immersed in the waters of adversity.

For instance, it is hard to watch others gather bushels of abundance while you gather the broken leftovers of a rich man's bounty one head at a time. Ruth teaches us it is hard not to compare the struggles of your lives with the good deals God seems to give other people. While we grub through our dull routines from sunup to sundown, we wonder why others do so little and yet are rewarded for their lack of commitment.

David supports this claim in Psalm 37. He tells us to take our eyes off the behavior of those who do wrong and seem to get away with evil. Actually they may *get by,* but they never *get away* with doing bad. Their action will eventually catch up with them. There is a natural tendency to get upset at the success of evil people, especially when their immoral life creates hardships for others. Remember, it is not for you to make that determination. Their outcome has already been determined. So the next time you compare your life to that of those who do wrong, remember their future is decided. "For like the grass they will soon wither, like green plants they will soon die away" (Ps. 37:2). The success of the superficial is not to be envied. They never fare well in the trials of life. Having no deep roots, they shrivel at the first signs of testing.

Let Ruth's focus be yours. Train your eye on the promises given to you by God. As you start over, "Trust in the LORD and do good" and—in time—"he will give you the desires of your heart" (Ps. 37:3–4). Ruth and David are joined in a common philosophy. Never envy the wicked, but trust in the Lord who supplies you with what you need. You should do good instead of imitating the evil habits of the wicked. If you do what is morally correct, God will give you the desires of your heart.

The believer should trust in the Lord. This is how Eugene Peterson translates these verses: "Get insurance with God and do a good deed, settle down and stick to your last. Keep company with God, get in on the best." When you trust God, you have an irrevocable assurance policy.

Ruth found out there is nothing inherently virtuous about being poor. David is right, "Better the little that the righteous have than the wealth of many wicked" (Ps. 37:16). This proverb was written centuries after Ruth went to Bethlehem, but it speaks of a day when Ruth was there, and it speaks to us in our day. If Ruth could speak to competitive Americans, she would probably say, "Lay aside your race to win in the marketplace. Quit grubbing and competing just to gain the wealth of the wicked. You are wrong when you assume there is any virtue in being poor or any esteem in being rich."

Ruth followed the harvesters. Of course she knew wealth can improve life. Everyone wants to have it better. But Ruth also learned in the fields that God is the owner of everything, and she was simply the manager. The wise steward learns that "the earth is the LORD's, and everything in it, the world, and all who live in it" (Ps. 24:1).

My mother walked in the way of Ruth. Her Bethlehem was the inner city. She grubbed for grace on the sidewalks of an impassionate city. She gleaned in the ghettos to feed her children. Like Ruth she learned there is no need to grub for the grace that God had already graciously provided for her.

Still my mother did it well. Fridays at the West house was a day of festivity. My mother flipped hamburgers or cooked fish. Often she invited the neighborhood friends to feast at our table. Dinner was purchased with food stamps. Still my mother opened the doors of our home in hospitality to many others. I would challenge my mother on why she gave away our little to others who appeared to have more than we did. She would say to me that she hoped someone would care for her children if they were hungry and away from home.

I recall the "grad" meals at the West house and the words of my mother who often had to grub and dig around in borrowed fields. I was clueless at the time that the providence of God was working behind the scenes. But today the words of William Cowper have new meaning to me:

God moves in a mysterious way
His wonders to perform;
He plants His footsteps in the sea
And rides upon the storm.

As Ruth moved in and out of the fields, she picked up every broken head of grain. I imagine she sang her own Magnificat, like Mary sang at the announcement and birth of Jesus. Praising God in the hard seasons is the only way to gain the Lord for all seasons. Ruth had no song in the bitter, barren lands of Moab. But here in the fields of Bethlehem Ruth's heart swelled with appreciation as she gleaned in the fields. Providentially God had leftovers in the field as a sign of His grace.

Ruth would soon learn that to praise God in the hard seasons is to gain a God for all seasons. The Bible tells about many fellow strugglers who serve as examples for the difficult times we face. Praising God is not a superfluous exercise. It is a conscious decision to worship God intentionally without regard to circumstance. Put a song in your heart as you face your hard times, and "let the word of Christ dwell in you richly as you teach and admonish one another with all wisdom, and as you sing psalms, hymns and spiritual songs with gratitude in your hearts to God" (Col. 3:16).

Ruth would soon commit to the God of Israel. She was a foreigner attempting the ways of the Hebrews. Even though she was once married to a Hebrew, Ruth eventually pledged her allegiance to this invisible reality named Jehovah. Ruth was learning that God is indeed a God for all seasons. In the winter of death, God blankets us with His comfort. In the spring of life, God makes everything new. Ruth would come to know in the heat of the summer that God would give her shade to bask in. These gifts are not exclusive to Ruth; they are acts of benevolence to us as well.

Whose Woman Is This?

"Boaz asked the foreman of his harvesters, 'Whose young woman is that?'" (Ruth 2:5). Boaz's name means "in him is strength."

Who is Ruth indeed? We have met her, and yet we have not spent the time to get to know her. Consider her biographical sketch. Ruth was a Moabite girl. She was married to Mahlon, an Israelite transplant. Ruth was the daughter-in-law of Naomi. And Ruth was like a breath of fresh air to her embittered mother-in-law. Ruth barnacled herself to Naomi in spite of her inability to produce another son for her to marry. Even if Naomi could have had another son, Ruth would have been ready for the geriatric ward by then. Ruth was a gleaner. Ruth by grace married Boaz. Ruth gave birth to a baby boy named Obed. Ruth was the grandmother of King David. Ruth miraculously was the great grandmother of Jesus. Not bad for a girl who started out as an adjective.

This was an impressive resume for a girl born on the wrong side of the tracks. The purpose of a biographical sketch is to provide information to help us know who Ruth is. Connect the lines and her brief might read like this: Ruth is God's woman, and any man who desires a real woman should want God to have her first. We are our best selves only when we belong first to God.

This happens when you become a person of God and a person for God. A woman's intimacy develops fully when she gives herself to God in prayer and faith. Relationships struggle when they are given on the horizontal level before they are given on the vertical level. You were made to give yourself first to the Gracious One who created you. When a woman champions her heavenly Father before she is sane enough to choose an earthly mate, the union is made in heaven. Only then is she ready to display agape to her companion.

Ruth's hard times of grubbing for grain finally ended in a season of sexual freedom and rich abundance, as defined in Proverbs 31. Interestingly, according to the Hebrew Bible, the book of Ruth follows the wisdom writings of Proverbs. This seems to suggest that when Solomon, author of many of the Proverbs, was looking for an illustration of a virtuous woman, he selected the life of Ruth.

Conversely, Proverbs 31 is a portrait of Mrs. Wonderful. But she develops into this noble character through stringent discipline. She is summed up in one statement, "She is worth far more than rubies. Her husband has full confidence in her and lacks nothing of value" (Prov. 31:10–11). Nineteen staccato statements describe how she became this woman of imperial character. Her nobility is won through the hard work of caring for her household from morning until evening. This portrait may be viewed by some as less than wonderful. But virtue is characterized as a person giving the essence of himself or herself to another.

Ruth learned a greater secret—to be a person of nobility is never easy, and developing character is seldom a regal process. If Ruth one day stands as queen of virtue, it is because she bent her back in gleaning. Ruth's right to speak on human virtue was won in the fields of Boaz. Ruth was in the process of becoming an icon of grace, and the process of becoming is always hard. There is nothing easy about God's development process. Discipline, determination, and a good dream are the steps to triumph. Again, had Ruth known the words of William

Cowper, she might have sung them in the difficult days when God was forging her character in the dust of Bethlehem. It would have been her anthem for the gleaners. And what an anthem!

Judge not the Lord by feeble sense,
But trust Him for His grace;
Behind a frowning providence
He hides a smiling face.

The harmony of an anthem is better sung when many voices blend together. If misery loves company, so does mercy. Thankfully, Ruth is not alone in fulfilling the purposes of God. Especially, as an outsider, Ruth discovered the ways of Israel's God. On the other hand, there was a biblical person named Esther who was an insider, and she also learned the ways in which God will and will not act. Their lives are similar because they achieved the will of God.

Ruth and Esther are the only women in the Bible who have books named after them. Ruth is the story of a Gentile who married Boaz, a Jew, and became a relative of the Messiah. "Salmon the father of Boaz, whose mother was Rahab, Boaz the father of Obed, whose mother was Ruth, Obed the father of Jesse, and Jesse the father of King David" (Matt. 1:5–6). Esther, on the other hand, was a Jew who married a Gentile and preserved the Jewish nation from destruction so Messiah could be born.

The story of Ruth begins with the famine in Bethlehem and ends with the birth of a baby. On the other hand, the story of Esther begins with a festival and ends with 75,000 deaths. Both stories deal with the grace and providence of God. God is mentioned twenty-five times in the book of Ruth. But in the story of Esther the name of God is not mentioned once. Clearly, in both historical narratives, God is seen on every page. For example, Mordecai, like Naomi, understood that Esther had been with God, just as Ruth had. Mordecai knew Esther was faithful and loyal to those who loved God. We see the purposes of God in the lives of these two courageous young women. Therefore, if you need a model on how to trust God in the face of famine, death, and feast, I recommend that you read the story of Ruth.

Ruth teaches us that the Lord can fill us with new hope for the future, in spite of misfortune and emptiness. Ruth also informs our faith to rely on the sweetness of God when life has turned bitter. Additionally, Ruth serves as a reminder that our present problems are as nothing when compared to God's fulfilled promises. Finally, Ruth demonstrates how God can transcend the hurts caused by death. In the shadow of death the light shines through. When baby Obed was born and given to Naomi, her bitterness was turned to sweetness. And death was conquered by life.

In both narratives Ruth and Esther sing the anthem of joy in the hard times of life. Esther learned the lyrics of God's grace from her earliest beginnings. Ruth had to learn how to shape the words of grace on her lips and life, as she moved forward in knowing God. Ruth and Esther experienced the will of God by standing close to their God and their men.

There is something dignified about women who have the ability to stand by their man, especially when the man has acted less than virtuously. Such an act of redeeming love was captured in an article in *Essence* magazine: This is a love story. The biography reads, "Cookie Johnson, wife of famed NBA basketball legend Magic Johnson, has been at his side through the best of times and the worst of times."

Cookie has loved Magic since their freshman year at Michigan State. She waited more than ten years to marry him. Still the road to the marriage altar was bumpy. Cookie and Magic first got engaged in 1985, but Magic just couldn't go through with the wedding. According to the article, "He broke out in hives, and he couldn't even play for a couple of games. Magic broke the engagement over the phone and Cookie was devastated."

They didn't speak for a year. "Then Magic called out of the blue one day when he was playing a game in Detroit. Cookie let him know she was seeing someone else, which drove him crazy. By the late eighties they were back together again, and she decided against her better judgment to move to Los Angeles."

By 1990, Cookie and Magic were engaged again. She had the dress hanging in the closet, and the invitations were in a corner waiting to be mailed. Magic called and said, "I can't do it." She said, "I'm not going to let you do this again." Magic asked for his ring back. Cookie said, "You can postpone the wedding, but you're staying engaged and you're going to get married." Determined, Cookie said, "No, we're not breaking up. We're going to continue being what we were."

When Magic said he was finally ready, Cookie refused to plan anything after so many disappointments. "If you're serious, you plan the wedding." And Magic did. They got married in Lansing, Michigan, on September 14, 1991.

Weeks later while they were still honeymooning, Magic got the news that would reshape their lives. Magic and Cookie announced to the world that he had contracted the HIV virus that causes AIDS. Somehow, the moment Cookie Johnson heard the crushing news herself, she summoned up a depth of love and forgiveness that would elude the most faithful of souls, and she did it on reflex, she says, without thinking twice. Cookie refused to ask how Magic became infected; she supported him during their difficult time. Cookie was pregnant with their unborn baby. Fortunately, she and the child were untouched by the disease.

The questions circled the air like buzzards waiting to pick its prey apart. What answer would this newlywed give to the critics who were looking suspiciously at her? But Cookie's answer embarrasses the love of many who say their love is eternal. "It was because of love," she explains with the quiet matter-of-factness her husband relies on. "I love him, and I knew he loved me." The godly woman stands by her man because he is "bone of my bones and flesh of my flesh" (Gen. 2:23).

Chapter Four

The Plus Factor
RUTH 2:8–18

Naomi—a woman made noble by her need. Naomi—a widow aching for the closeness she once knew in marriage. She was poor and worse than poor. She was a minus in this world's equation. She was penniless, childless, hopeless, and alone. The mathematics of her deplorable state had reduced her to one plus nothing. When Naomi added to her barren economy, all she knew was her total assets, and her total assets equaled zero.

But let us remember this: Before any zero in any one-plus-zero equation is the plus sign. To live beneath God's grace is to live beneath the cross—

and Christ's cross is your plus sign. G. K. Chesterton said, "The cross cannot be defeated for it is defeat." Christ died to become your unfailing friend. He added the plus sign to the terror of facing the world alone. You are never quite against the world uncompanioned. It is always "you-plus," and the plus sign is God's invitation to add the Gracious One's own presence in the configuration of your survival.

Then Boaz said to Ruth, "You will listen, my daughter, will you not? Do not go to glean in another field, nor go from here, but stay close by my young women. Let your eyes be on the field which they reap, and go after them. Have I not commanded the young men not to touch you? And when you are thirsty, go to the vessels and drink from what the young men have drawn." So she fell on her face, bowed down to the ground, and said to him, "Why have I found favor in your eyes, that you should take notice of me, since I am a foreigner?" And Boaz answered and said to her, "It has been fully reported to me, all that you have done for your mother-in-law since the death of your husband, and how you have left your father and your mother and the land of your birth, and have come to a people whom you did not know before. The LORD repay your work, and

a full reward be given you by the LORD God
of Israel, under whose wings you have come
for refuge." Then she said, "Let me find favor
in your sight, my lord; for you have com-
forted me, and have spoken kindly to your
maidservant, though I am not like one of
your maidservants." Now Boaz said to her at
mealtime, "Come here, and eat of the bread,
and dip your piece of bread in the vinegar."
So she sat beside the reapers, and he passed
parched grain to her; and she ate and was
satisfied, and kept some back. And when
she rose up to glean, Boaz commanded
his young men, saying, "Let her glean even
among the sheaves, and do not reproach
her. Also let grain from the bundles fall pur-
posely for her; leave it that she may glean,
and do not rebuke her." . . . So she gleaned
in the field until evening, and beat out what
she had gleaned, and it was about an ephah
of barley. Then she took it up and went into
the city, and her mother-in-law saw what she
had gleaned. So she brought out and gave
to her what she had kept back after she had
been satisfied (Ruth 2:8–18 NKJV).

Come with me to the barley fields of Bethlehem,
1100 B.C. It is the season of the barley harvest. God
is about to add a huge plus factor to the life of a

disenfranchised widow. The barley has been freshly cut. The scent of new grain lingers in the air as the reapers gather about Boaz of Bethlehem to dump their baskets into his sweet-smelling granaries.

Enter Boaz. Boaz was rich, independent, and valiant. He was the very picture of the farm manager of the year. He felt God had given him all. His life reflected the full measure of heaven's abundance. There was nothing God could add to him. Then suddenly his world was upside down. The world was full of violins. Cupid fired an arrow—and whammo! The arrow landed in the center of Boaz's heart. It bled the liquid of passion. Into his rich fields stepped a beautiful young woman. She was poor and in tatters, but she was a kind of empress who owned the day.

Ruth, the ragged queen of the barley harvest, was pleasant as she made her way into the field. Meticulously, Ruth entered the field following the counsel of her mother-in-law, Naomi. Ruth had earlier pled with her, "Where you go I will go, and where you stay, I will stay. Your people will be my people and your God my God" (see Ruth 1:16). Now Naomi had encouraged Ruth to go to the field to glean the fallen grain missed by the harvesters. But Naomi also wanted her to take precautions among the reapers because some of these harvest ruffians molested single women, especially the widows, who were destitute and unprotected.

Ruth entered the field. The heads of the men swiveled in her direction as they paused momentarily to take a glance at this quiet, attractive young woman. Ruth gained permission from the straw boss to come into the field and glean among the harvesters. The reapers, according to Levitical law, were not to glean all of the field but to leave enough behind so poor people would have something to survive on.

So Ruth entered the fields. She groveled in the hard earth, picking up the broken heads of grain. Quietly without any word of warning Boaz was at her side—no, more than that, he was in her life. Boaz was a young man of wealth. He walked with the demeanor of a soldier; yet he was a person of strength and encouragement. Stunned by Ruth's beauty, he asked the field hands, "Who is this woman and who does she belong to?"

Boaz was told that Ruth was a widow who had recently come to Israel, having left Moab. Boaz discovered Ruth had accompanied Naomi, who had returned to Bethlehem, and he knew that she was a good worker. The field hands pointed out that Ruth had worked from morning until now and had taken only a short break before returning to gather the stalks of barley. Boaz was intrigued. This poor but lovely woman was a portrait of hope and promise. Yet there seemed to be a stealthy demon that stalked this woman.

Ruth's poverty had caused her to cower in fear before the owner of the field. There was a sense in which neither of them could brag about their "high-born" past. Boaz might have been rich, but he had a rather checkered past. His mother was a prostitute by the name of Rahab. Ruth was a gentle widow—with issues about her past. Boaz sensed her loneliness. Ruth was a person who had abandoned not only her past but her loyalties to her past. She looked back at him and had to admit that Boaz was a "handsome hunk." *He is rich, and I am poor,* she thought. *Boaz would never look twice at me.* Ruth abandoned hope.

Ruth was so poor, so alone, so far down on herself that she could not see the plus factor. But the plus factor is always available. God is at every moment able to add to our destitution. Such was the case with other biblical women—Sarah, Rachel, and Hannah. Each woman was remembered for her barrenness. Their impoverished condition was the entrée for God's plus factor. To Sarah, God gave Isaac, to Rachel God added Joseph, and to Hannah God blessed with Samuel.

Boaz counseled Ruth to glean as much as she wished in his fields. "Glean all you want. Don't forget as you work in the field; stay very close to those who work for me." Boaz had, unknown to Ruth, given instructions to the field hands who worked for him, "Make sure no one molests her. Be very clear that no one takes advantage of her. Give her the freedom to work. She is family, in a way. She is the daughter-in-law of Naomi and my deceased relative, Elimelech."

As they talked, Ruth summons up her courage and dared to speak to this Bethlehem plantation owner. "My Lord, what have I done to gain such favor from you, and where does this favor come from? How did I gain it and why would you pay attention to me, since I'm no more than a foreigner, a poor vagabond gleaning in your field?"

Astonishingly, God's plus factor was operative in the life of Ruth. Lurking behind this story stands the hand of God that is operative in every intricate detail of Ruth's life. A German proverb declares, "Begin to weave, and God will give the thread." What is true of Ruth is true of us. God is involved in our lives even when we think he is absent. There is a great big plus factor standing over all our needs. Think you are forgotten? Nonsense! James Russell Lowell describes the plus factor this way:

Truth forever on the scaffold,
    wrong forever on the throne.
Yet that scaffold sways the future,
    and behind the dim unknown,
Standeth God within the shadow,
    keeping watch above his own.

It is piteous when you are caught up in the scheme of things and think you are alone. How false! God is there orchestrating every act. You may not see God's hand. Many times you cannot even feel God's presence. You may wonder from time to time, *Am I really a part of God's unfolding redemptive drama?* Take heart; you have a plus factor. God is there between the alpha and the omega, disclosing all that the Generous One is and what He wants to do. God will guide this journey. Jehovah-Jireh provides the road map.

Ruth and Boaz began a simple exchange. Boaz said several things that later we can attribute to the plus factor, because the plus factor is little more than God keeping His promises. One such thing Boaz said to Ruth was that she was to glean in the fields with the young women. He gave Ruth a kind of provision. Boaz supplied her need because he knew Ruth had cared so deeply for her mother-in-law. This condition of agreement is clear in the story. It's not Boaz providing for Ruth; it's God supporting Ruth in keeping with her own testament to Naomi when she pledged her allegiance, "Your God shall be my God." In that moment of allegiance, God bound Himself to the life of Ruth. Yahweh did for a Gentile what He had always done for the children of Israel. God had been the constant contributor for the Hebrews, and now He would also be a donor even for young Ruth. Why would God do this? Because He is an equal opportunity God. It is all of grace, and grace is God honoring the plus factor in our lives.

Are we really any different from Ruth? Do we not desperately depend upon the provisions of God? But many of Christ's followers have a tendency to speak of God in purely material terms. Christians may be the most clearly marked by this obsession. Often God is seen as the cosmic Santa Claus who provides those who are nice with bigger houses, fashionable clothing, or expensive cars. Jesus warns us against this world's possessions: "Watch out! Be on your guard against all kinds of greed; a man's life does not consist in the abundance of his possessions" (Luke 12:15). Therefore, we should proceed with caution, so as not to assume that the blessings of God are limited to tangibles. The tragic assumption is that paraphernalia are the only blessings of God—more of the same possessions you already have. Thus, God becomes secondary, and money, houses, and cars become the new Trinity. The authentic provisions of God run much deeper. They are hidden.

Boaz said to Ruth, "Go out and glean in the field. Gather the fallen grain along with my women." Then Boaz gave Ruth a measure of extra protection by saying to his young men, "Don't bother her." He understood the rapacious nature of young men who felt their testosterone levels rising as they watched young women working in the fields.

We cannot know how Boaz really looked. He may not have been a "love god," but he was a godly man who looked at Ruth as a real human being. Boaz valued Ruth as a woman. He did not devalue her; neither did he allow anyone else to humiliate her. Boaz didn't reduce Ruth down to some sexual unit. Ruth was a woman, one of God's wonderful creations that ought never to be injured, abused, or mistreated.

Some women in our day have been so mentally, psychologically, and physically abused that they have become immune to the pain, embracing it as their common way of life. Thankfully, God knows better, and so do we. Boaz actually gave a loving provision and a caring protection for the life of this woman, and Ruth was overwhelmed by his grace. "Why in this world have you been so kind to me?" she asked.

Kindness becomes the driving tone of the entire story. It is what the Hebrews call *hesed*—going beyond the call of duty, going a step further than what is required. Boaz was a cousin of Elimelech. Now he attached himself to his kinsperson's widow, Naomi. Boaz made himself responsible when he said to Ruth: "I show this above-and-beyond responsibility because it has been noticed throughout the community all that you have done for your mother-in-law, how you left your home, how you abandoned your own mother and father, how you left your own religion, your understandings of the supernatural, and you have followed Naomi and cherished her

God as your God. Now because of your treatment of Naomi, I, in turn, give kindness back to you."

Grace—it's all of grace! *Hesed* is going above and beyond the responsibilities that are required.

Boaz knew the meaning of grace. He understood that *hesed* is the plus factor. He invited Ruth to drink deeply of this *hesed*. "Get you some water whenever you get thirsty and drink from the well which my men draw from . . . go out and glean in the field and gather your goods." Then Boaz looked over at his field hands and told them of the plus factor. "When she goes out among the unbundled sheaves to collect her barley, don't scold her; don't tell her that she's doing it all wrong. Ruth has been scolded and beaten enough in life. Let her gather whatever she needs."

Then Boaz added a further plus factor. "As she collects the grain, deliberately drop some barley. Make sure that you intentionally leave a lot extra so Ruth can gather in abundance—so she and Naomi will have enough to survive. Do this every day throughout the harvest."

The plus factor is always the way God thrusts His hand into our lives. At no time has God given you just what you need. "Now to him who is able to do immeasurably more than all we ask or imagine, according to his power that is at work within us" (Eph. 3:20). God has always given you more than you need. To beg God for your daily bread is to find that He always adds dessert.

God adds the pluses even when the minuses seem to dominate our lives. Maybe Boaz was able to give a plus factor because he had experienced the margins of pain in life. Possibly Boaz had lived through a season of great hurt. There are always some minuses in life. Maybe you too were born in some peculiar or obscure way. Maybe you have grown up in some abject circumstances. Perhaps others have looked down on you because you are the wrong color or the wrong sex or you have the wrong education or the wrong political affiliation. Perhaps they have minimized your self-worth to the point that you always see a minus in front of your being. Yet God is always transforming your minuses with his plus signs.

Robert Schuller was asked why he always talked about "possibility thinking" and didn't preach the cross. Schuller rejected this proposition and replied that he always preached the cross. His approach to preaching the cross as well as the doctrine of redemption was contextualized to fit the situation of the California culture. The Crystal Cathedral would empty if he preached the cross in its blaring truth. He explained to his critics they should never assume he is not preaching the reality of the cross. Schuller understands the cross as the story of God taking the minuses of our life and turning them into plus signs.

This is why we call Christ's horrible black Friday a Good Friday. We rejoice over the fact that

God can turn the minuses of any Friday into a plus by the following resurrection Sunday. Indeed, this is why we assemble as the community of faith—to allow the God of *hesed* to change the minuses of our lives into plusses.

The Bible is a long account of such pluses and minuses. Job lived as a man who was upright. As a father, Job regularly interceded for his family. He looked unfavorably on evil. His eyes were constantly on the goodness of God. But Job lived through a season of catastrophe. A major part of his life was minuses. The dirge of loss played as an anthem in Job's world. Still, all his debits were at last changed to credits.

Joseph also lived in the minuses of life. Joseph was the darling of his father's heart. To look at Joseph was to find the face of Jacob's beloved wife, Rachel. Joseph's life took a shift from the warmth of his father's house to the bottom of a cold, empty cistern. Down the spiral, the downward motion continued because he was sold into slavery. Further down, Joseph slid into the dungeon, the state prison. He was jailed on trumped-up charges. Yet he ended up on a pinnacle of pluses.

Ruth came to see that God gives pluses to life. "Let her eat," said Boaz to the men. Then he said to her, "As we break away from everything, I want you to come to my village tent and sit down with us for supper." Ruth answered the invitation. She sat and she ate and ate and ate until she was satisfied. Ruth ate and remembered the purpose for which she went into the harvest field. She did not go into the fields just to work for herself. She did this for Naomi as well. Ruth was a woman living under oath. She had made a promise to Naomi: "Where you go, I go. And where you live, I will live. Your people will be my people. Your God shall be my God. And where you die, I shall die."

Ruth kept her promise with broken heads of barley gleaned in the blazing heat of the day. Boaz took notice and committed himself to further filling her "doggie bag" each night. He didn't have to ask Ruth why she was taking carry-out with her. He knew it was not for Ruth's midnight snack. She had already been satisfied. Ruth was filling her bags to make sure her mother-in-law would have something to eat as well.

Whenever you tap into God's plus factor, you understand it is a bonus in your life. So you are always willing to share it with someone less fortunate than you. God's plus factor always centers on human decency. This happens only when we understand that all we have comes from the abundance of the magnificent hands of God. If you assume your good fortune emanates from another place, chances are you will withhold your possessions. On the other hand, the intuitive person is aware that the extras in his life are bonuses from God.

This spirit of sharing rarely comes from people of great means. Ruth had nothing. She was dirt poor. Ruth was living between a loaf of barley and the grave. So her kindness did not come from the generosity of a wealthy woman. Ruth gave out of her poverty.

Like Ruth, you may have supplied out of your poverty. Consider those who live in humble houses with barely enough to feed their own family, and watch Daddy have the nerve to feed someone down the street. You feel a flash of momentary anger? There you are living off leftovers with barely enough to eat between the night and the next day. Inquisitively your mother asks, "Are you hungry?" Indignantly you feel like saying, "Woman, are you for real! Everybody in our little world is hungry." But when you live on the plus factor of life, you cannot keep what you have to yourself. You are always looking to share what you have with someone else. This is the time when God dumps into your life a whole truckload of *hesed.*

Ruth toiled on for the sake of her mother-in-law, Naomi. She was beaten by groveling in the dirt for broken barley heads. But at last the day was done mercifully. What wonderful respite! Sleep . . . "Sleep," said the Bard, "that knits the raveled sleeve of care." The sun was about to set. Ruth left the fields to head home where she hoped to fill Naomi's empty stomach. Reentering the story is Naomi.

Ruth's mother-in-law actually asked her a couple of questions. Obviously, there was nothing passive in what she asked. "Where have you gleaned today? And who took notice of you?"

Ruth answered Naomi, "I was noticed by a man of substance. He gingerly approached me to engage me in conversation. He was attentive to my every movement. When I disclosed myself to him, he hung on to my every word. His eyes were full of compassion as he asked me my name. The man talked to me as if he had made some inquiry about who I was. He was very kind. His name was Boaz."

When Naomi heard this she commented to her daughter-in-law, "Blessed be he of the Lord, who has not forsaken His kindness to the living and the dead . . . This man is a relation of ours, one of our close relatives" (Ruth 2:20 NKJV). The term *kinsman-redeemer* is introduced to the plot. Naomi was saying, "God has been kind not just to us who are now living, but Yahweh has remembered His relationship to His family throughout time. Because of Elimelech, God has shown kindness to you, Ruth."

Within the dialogues between Ruth and Boaz and Naomi and Ruth, you sense what the plus factor is all about. The plus factor is the lingering note of *hesed* that sounds throughout the life of Ruth and Naomi. There are three words that stand out— praise, encouragement, and redemption.

Praise

We are to praise God because He has remembered us and not abandoned us. Some people say, "I don't need anybody but Jesus." While this sounds pious, it is not entirely true. Neither is loneliness realistic. In truth, we need each other. "No man is an island, entire of itself," said John Donne. "Every man is a piece of the continent, a part of the main. Any man's death diminishes me . . . therefore never send to know for whom the bell tolls; it tolls for thee."

We were not created to live in isolation. We are designed to live in community with one another. It is because of our love for Jesus that we treat others the way we want God to care about us. We cannot live long or well by ourselves. Everything we eat, what we drink or wear are a compilation of many hands working together to make it possible for us to survive. We do not live by ourselves. We all live in concert with one another.

Spirituality is not our invitation to start bragging, "I don't need anybody else." There are times when you need a friend to talk to, an ear to listen to you, a shoulder to lean on, or a hand to hold. "And let us consider how we may spur one another on toward love and good deeds. Let us not give up meeting together, as some are in the habit of doing, but let us encourage one another—and all the more as you see the Day approaching" (Heb. 10:24–25).

Praise to God for remembering us is not to be conducted only by ourselves. Public worship is important to our spiritual maturity. Notice that praise is not limited to structures of worship. Praise has much to do with partnership. The story of Ruth reminds us of the power of companionship.

"If you would reap praise you must sow the seeds: gentle words and useful deeds."

—Anonymous

Encouragement

Encouragement is another key word in this story. Ruth's entire life becomes a venture of faith. God is there with the undergirding, this embracing, of a man who is her kinsman-redeemer. This relative takes notice of a young woman who is out in the fields by herself. Boaz moves beyond his own self-interest into the interest of another. This is what encouragement is at its best. It is giving strength to those who are weak. It is God, after all, who lifts us up. He puts wind beneath our wings. God is the One who cares for all compassionately.

Boaz made a great statement when he said, "God will pay you back. God will give you wages! God will put the wind beneath your wings." God is in the business of encouraging. He clothes us with steel when we can't stand life's pressures by ourselves. Too often the vocabulary of the church is *self-sufficiency.* We have imitated Wall Street. The church parrots the patent phrases of many commercial slogans. Sadly, we have not experienced *hesed.* Eventually, there is a defining moment in every person's life. This is a time when you should move beyond the comfort level to encourage someone else. When you start encouraging others your problems won't look so big to you anymore.

Encouragement. All of us need it. No matter the success you have achieved in life, you still need encouragement. Some people today may be trying to make some big decision. Life is tumbling down. You are in anguish. You cry, "What am I going to do? How did I get where I am? What went wrong?" You need encouragement. C. H. Spurgeon said, "Even when you cannot trace God's hand, learn how to trust God's heart." The Gracious One knows exactly what you need, and God knows just how much you can bear.

Redemption

Boaz was Naomi's kinsman-redeemer, the one who would pay back and buy back all that belonged to her late husband. Naomi recognized that Boaz was not merely a relative; he was a close relative.

Closeness means that Boaz lived under the Leviticus code. According to the code, Boaz was her kinsman-redeemer who must buy back Naomi's lost fortune to restore dignity, worth, and value to her life.

Men, this is a place where you and I become very strong for our women. We are to be careful not to degrade, devalue, or demote women. Regardless of what women have done or how they have behaved, they are our queens. God has put on us a demand that we are to value what they need and respect who they are. Sisters, rejoice when you receive the esteem of your man. Never become haughty, as though you are entitled to your imaginary throne. When the church lifts you up, do not gloat as though you were born to enjoy the prestige.

We are all debtors—but to God only. We all owe God something! And it is because we men owe God everything that we also owe our women something. And our work is all to be given so we can be the persons God has called us to be. And just because a man may have substance, wealth, and influence gives him no right to use his position to control or abuse a woman.

Naomi told Ruth, "It is good that you go on out and work in the field of this particular man." Naomi did not mention God, but she knew Ruth had not accidentally wound up in the field of Boaz. Naomi knew if Ruth was in the right place at the right time, meeting the right person, God had arranged it all. That kind of secure existence is an evidence of His plus factor. God is always up to something and always outdoing Himself. When you think you own the blessing of God, sit down and strap yourself in. You ain't seen nothing yet.

In the spring semester of 1979, Norman Johnson's son, Bryon, complained about a stomachache. Initially there was no need for alarm. Children often suffer from abdominal pains. Attempts were made by the Johnsons to relieve their son of the pains. But when the pain turned chronic, Norman and his wife Lois took their bundle of joy to the hospital. At first the doctors could not find anything wrong with Bryon. Still the aches did not subside. Medical specialists were called in, and a battery of tests were given. A malignant tumor was located in the stomach. Some time later Bryon was diagnosed with leukemia.

Norman informed our homiletics class about the condition of his son and asked if we would pray for his family and his son. He also asked our class to give the gift of life. The entire class responded and gave blood for our fellow student's son. The kinship surrounding the event welded us into a family. Bryon had become our son as well.

Norman and Lois moved into Parkland Hospital, each exchanging shifts without complaint. The Johnsons never imposed on anyone who offered to stay at the hospital in order for him and his wife to get rest. Norman never reneged on his university studies, nor did he complain. Much of the time he suffered alone, and the rest of us never really knew how much he suffered. He would leave class, go to the hospital, stay around the clock, then go to his secular job and work around the clock. Then, to add horror to his troubled life, the doctor came in one night and said to Norman, "Mr. Johnson, your son has a 99 percent chance of not living. Furthermore, Mrs. Johnson, you will never be able to have another child."

The day after the doctor's news was Norman's assigned preaching day. He read his text and announced his subject, "God and One Percent." Norman heralded the mighty truth which is at the center of the book of Ruth. We are not alone. Norman and Ruth remind us, "Sometimes life is a downer! Everything points to can't, ain't, won't, impossible. The doctor reads your ultimatum. You have a one percent chance to live. When you get the news of doom, add God to your gloom. You still have the possibility of pulling it off. God plus one is all it takes."

Unfortunately, Norman's son died. But Lois conceived and gave birth to a daughter. By the way, Norman's daughter has graduated from college and his son is growing into young adulthood. The doctor had told Norman, "Your wife will never be able to have another child." First came a daughter, and the church prayed until they had a son.

Boaz and Ruth learned the same plus factor—but it is yours as well. You are never alone. It is always God plus one. God can pull it off.

Countless persons have experienced the overwhelming generosity of God. For those who have experienced God's mercy, report the news—God and one percent is enough for a miracle. To those in need of encouragement, give God your one percent and watch the Gracious One work. Also, to those in need of redemption, God has a kinsman-redeemer who has purchased your deliverance. Those of you who need to praise God for being God, celebrate the Generous One and this truth—with one percent plus God, you can make it.

Jesus is in the plus-factor business. He cries out to your despair. Not enough means? Nonsense! Bring the fish and bread to Me. How many fish do you have? Just two fish and a few loaves of bread? It's more than enough. Then stand back and watch the plus factor come into your needy life.

Chapter Five

Life's Interludes of Uncertainty

RUTH 2:19–23

Anita stopped by the house of her good neighbor the other morning. Almost from the moment she walked though the door, she launched into one of those long, soulful conversations that occasionally come between friends as a gift.

Two years ago, Anita's brother died suddenly. Four months later her father died. And now, just before Christmas, her mother, who had been in good health, died after developing pneumonia.

Right now, Anita just prays for a period of calm in her life. What she is clamoring for is an interlude—a period of rest between the highly active performances in her life's drama. Interlude is a term often used in dramatic performances when a play takes a rest from the intense moments in a literary piece. Additionally, it is the period of an unresolved plot.

The story of Ruth slows down to savor the uncertain moments surrounding her adventure. Up to this point, Ruth's life has been filled with one highly charged event after another. Consider the intense vignettes surrounding her life. After Ruth's marriage ended abruptly, she was faced with the decision of whether to stay in her country or relocate to Bethlehem—a land foreign to her. Then Ruth accepted the God of her mother-in-law, Naomi. Now she must learn how to survive in a land different from her own. We can almost hear Ruth exhale and delight in the reality of one of life's interludes. Like Anita, Ruth takes a breather from the supercharged events in her spectacular life.

May the Lord Bless the Man Who Noticed You

Typically, mothers-in-law and daughters-in-law are at odds. At least that is the way mother-in-law and daughter-in-law relationships are often perceived. Yet, there is nothing typical or ordinary about the milieu of Naomi and Ruth's world. So we enter another extraordinary act performed by this exemplary mother-in-law, Naomi.

There is a unique benediction forming on the lips of Naomi. Actually, Naomi pronounced a blessing on her daughter-in-law. Naomi's prayer parallels the prayer of Ruth, "May your people be my people." Here Naomi echoed Ruth's request by granting her a world-altering benediction: "Bless the man who took notice of you!" The future of Ruth will start over in new and adventurous ways because of this blessing given by Naomi.

Naomi would not wait for a funeral to pronounce good words in Ruth's direction. There had been too many deaths and funerals already. Now was the time to posture for a festival. Unfortunately, many people have the opportunity to pronounce good on others, but they wait until it is too late. Today, announce to the person who noticed you a blessing to carry into the future.

The events of Naomi's past made her a bitter old woman. But she never displayed her bitterness toward Ruth. This is a wonderful picture that shatters the modern image of what mother-in-law/ daughter-in-law relationships are. Naomi was a mother to Ruth, and Ruth was a daughter to Naomi. The two women were family to each other. "Consequently, you are no longer foreigners and aliens, but fellow citizens with God's people and members of God's household" (Eph. 2:19).

Enlarging the size of the family is the business of God. Every addition to the family of God is a celebration. Like parents welcoming a newborn into the household, holding the baby in their arms, and cooing in the face of the child, so God smiles at us. It is God's enterprise to increase the family with the addition of children. From our first parents, Adam and Eve, to our present parents, God desires to include you in the family tree. Now that you are in the family of God, meet the relatives you don't know.

Read the names found in Matthew's genealogy of Jesus. The list of names includes the likes of Abraham, the father of the faithful, who risked the chastity of Sarah to save his own skin. Meet another relative on the family tree—David, a shepherd, poet, and king who also happened to be a stud. In between the two celebrity relatives you come across these names, "Salmon the father of Boaz, whose mother was Rahab, Boaz the father of Obed, whose mother was Ruth" (Matt. 1:5). God loves family, but you have no jurisdiction over whom Yahweh adds to the family tree.

The enlargement of family is the result of romance, and God is always behind the romance of His children. None of these relationships is an accident. He enjoys the connections of different people from various backgrounds coming together and creating new additions to His family. Consider your marriage to your beloved. Can you remember a time when you did not know each other? And how about the discoveries of your likes and dislikes? Eventually a romance stirred in the hearts of two unlikely candidates, and now you are a part of the "until death do us part" family.

Maybe you are single and are constantly reminded, "I am alone." You feel that if you had physical companionship your worries about the uncertain future would disappear. Remember, one is a whole number. You plus God makes the difference. This interlude can be a good time to start preparing to begin or to start over again. You can begin by creating space for spiritual intimacy with God or developing a devotional life. Giving yourself to ministry and serving God in the world is a good place for you to begin. Like Jesus and the apostle Paul, singleness can be a great place to align your will to the purposes of God.

This is just an interlude for you. Keep in mind the best of interludes are never left to uncertainty. It's easy to conclude that the Eternal One has forgotten about you. Slip into a "pity party" and go through life pouting. You say you are getting older and the biological clock is ticking. The tendency is to jump ahead of God. Consider that you may be in the interlude of your life's drama. Besides, uncertainty of the future is another way of "walking by faith and not by sight." The best of interludes are never left to chance.

A meticulous reading of the book of Ruth points to God on every page. Although the choices made by the head of the family clan led to death and bitterness, it also led to the establishment of a relationship that will lead to the grandparenting of the Messiah. The story of Ruth informs our faith, with God being involved in every minute detail of our existence.

Consequently, it is appropriate to say that God hides himself in human romance. God cares intently about romances. Read the Bible; it is filled with lofty love stories. The Bible begins with the love story of Adam and Eve. From their romance, the world's family was born. There is also the story of centenarian Abraham and geriatric Sarah literally making love and birthing the child of laughter.

Before us is another grand love story—Jacob the trickster. He was a man who manipulated his way through life, stealing and cheating. Then Jacob had to run for his life. He fled to the house of his uncle Laban, who happened to be a cunning man like Jacob. Then, Jacob fell in love with beautiful Rachel and was tricked into marrying her weak-eyed sister, Leah. In order to have Rachel's hand in marriage, Jacob had to work a total of fourteen years. Jacob worked tirelessly because he loved Rachel. From these unions the twelve tribes of Israel were born.

A final romance story is that of Mary, a virgin, and her fiancé, Joseph. He learned of her pregnancy and wished to break off the engagement without humiliating Mary. While trying to sleep, Joseph had a night visitor who informed him that Mary's pregnancy was a miracle of God. The Holy Spirit had conceived the child, and it was of God. Joseph resolved to go the full term of the pregnancy and submit himself to ridicule. He raised Jesus as his own son and never showed contempt. He loved Mary as his bride. Unfortunately Joseph is often a forgotten man at Christmas, but he is a champion for the cause of God's romance. God is a romantic, and He delights in the romance of His people.

The interlude in the love story of Ruth leaves us questioning the outcome of her future. Ruth identified the protagonist as the man who took notice of her—Boaz. Naomi then said, "The LORD bless him" (Ruth 2:20). A freer translation of Naomi's benediction might read, "Lord, make Boaz happy." Neither Naomi nor Ruth knew the full extent of this benediction.

In each of these narratives, the Holy Spirit was the mortar of godly romance. A careful rereading of each story reveals the Holy Spirit at work. It is the Holy Spirit who welds the heart together in human love. Without the Spirit at work in romance, you have only horizontal love—banal, prosaic love. When the Holy Spirit is added to the ingredient of romance, we learn that agape love originates with God. All the Harlequin romance novels pale in comparison when attempting to capture the romance generated in the human heart by the Holy Spirit.

Naomi's Benediction

The news about Boaz and his generosity caused Naomi to break out in praise to God. "The LORD bless him!" she declared, as she recognized Boaz's kindness. Moreover, Naomi was rejoicing and thinking about God: "He has not stopped showing his kindness to the living and the dead" (Ruth 2:20). God has not ceased showing kindness and faithfulness to the living—that is, to Naomi and Ruth. Neither had He postponed revealing His faithfulness to the dead. Once again, God disclosed His strong sense of family. And as a loving Father, God demonstrated kindness and faithfulness for Naomi and Ruth, as well as their dead husbands.

God always shows faithfulness toward those who live by faith and those who have died by faith. No one who has seen the action of the Lord can doubt that God goes on rewarding the faithful actions of those who trusted in Him all their lives.

For example, tourists take the trip to New York City, to the Hall of Fame, in order to commemorate the names of outstanding Americans. The persons inducted into this national shrine have been distinguished for their outstanding contributions in a particular profession or activity. The reading of these names stirs pride, appreciation, and sometimes suspicion in the observer. Often, the question about how some persons were inducted resonates.

Subsequently, you don't have to take a trip any further than the book of Hebrews. There you will make a turn to chapter 11 and find the "hall of fame of the faithful." Here you may linger and study the faces and read the biographies of the known greats in the faith as well as the honorable mentions. Each life teaches us, "Without faith it is impossible to please God, because anyone who comes to him must believe that he exists and that he rewards those who earnestly seek him" (Heb. 11:6).

- By faith Abel gave a better offering than his brother Cain.
- By faith Enoch walked the long way home and was beamed up to a heavenly address.
- By faith Noah built the ark when he had never seen or heard the word *rain.*
- By faith Abraham journeyed without a map and under sealed orders.
- By faith blind Isaac blessed his twins Jacob and Esau and gave to them a new future.
- By faith Jacob, who stole his blessing, now gives blessings away.
- By faith Moses was delivered from the Nile River and rescued Israel through the Red Sea.

By faith walls fell to ground zero. By faith Rahab became the great-grandmother of Jesus. And there are many more honorable mentions hanging on the wall of faith. Some mentioned there were warriors and prophets. Others were men and women of faith who met death head-on. Some were burned in the flames, some were eaten by lions, and others were sawed in two. Some were stoned, persecuted, mistreated, wandering around in sheep and goat skins, jeered, flogged—you name it, and it happened to these faithful. And the list goes on and on. Above the exit door of the hall are the words, "These were all commended for their faith; yet, none of them received what had been promised. God had planned something better for us so that only together with us would they be made perfect."

Today, these men and women of faith are the great cloud of witnesses. They are a huge collaboration of those who were martyred. They look down out of heaven and see the Christianity they died to promulgate roaring in life all around the world. Their faith is being rewarded even after they are dead.

I have the strong feeling that whatever my strong achievements are, my mother is cashing in on her faith in me. Like Naomi who pronounced a benediction on Ruth, I think of my own mother's prayers. Prayer is an intimate encounter and should not be intruded on by the irreverent. I used to watch my mother kneel by the side of her bed, and

I listened to her as she talked to God. She prayed for the oldest sibling to the youngest, naming the needs of each of her children. When she got to my name, it frightened the life out of me. Who wants the God of the universe turned loose on you? Yet, it was from those prayers that I believe I have cashed in on my mother's blessings.

I'm reflecting on my pastor who prayed the passion to preach in me. August 10, 1975, was the night of my first sermon. Before you went into the church each prospectus had to stop by the pastor's study. There Pastor O. C. Johnson Sr. had me kneel. Next he laid his hands on me and prayed for my future as a preacher. Along with his words, tears fell on my head. I have always believed that was a kind of transference of his anointing.

My mother's prayers and my pastor's blessing served as rites of passage. I learned there is an incredible amount of power released in us when we realize that others believe in us. This is the greatest power known. Faith in another person releases in him the power to become what he believes he can be.

In January of 1990 I sat in the east wing of the Crystal Cathedral during the Successful Church Leadership Conference. This was the year when Robert Schuller celebrated the twenty-fifth year of the conference. I relish every moment listening to the stories of churches I had never heard of and how God was blessing them. This was a crucial time for me because our church was facing the need to expand. Adjacent to our facility were seven acres of land, and I thought that was the amount of land we needed. Negotiations were in process while I was attending the conference. Immediately my vision shifted from seven acres as I listened to the stories of churches purchasing forty, sixty, and a hundred acres of land. I knew this was the place for me—to have my vision defined and my dreams enlarged.

Bill Hybels, senior pastor of Willow Creek Community Church, was scheduled to speak. Hybels began his afternoon presentation by telling the Willow Creek Church story, how he began in ministry and how his church was started. I was fascinated with his story. It had nothing to do with the size of Willow Creek Church; it was something Hybels said to me.

When Hybels organized Willow Creek, he asked Robert Schuller, who had a layover in Chicago, to stop in on his group and say a few words to his fellowship. Hybels said Bob didn't stay long or talk long. He stood and said, "Bill, I believe in you, and God believes in you too!" The conference ended for me after that statement. I had traveled from Texas to California to hear those words, "Ralph, I believe in you!" I wept uncontrollably when I heard those words. I had never been affirmed as a pastor. But that day the light was turned on and the darkness disappeared. At last, I knew that God believed in me. The power of belief is that we become what we believe. Faith of others in us releases the power to become what we believe we can be.

Naomi believed in Ruth, God, and her husband's relative. Boaz is "one of our kinsman-redeemers," she said. The term was foreign to Ruth, because she was not a native of Bethlehem. She had much to learn about the ways of Jehovah.

Kinsman-Redeemer

Naomi introduced a new hope to Ruth, just as our hope in Jesus Christ is our "hope of glory." The hope that the world clings to is a dead hope, but our hope is alive because it is grounded in Jesus Christ, our "living hope."

Naomi explained to Ruth the role and responsibility of the kinsman-redeemer (see Lev. 25:47–55). The confidence of Naomi was more than the kindness of Boaz or his love for Ruth. She had experienced the truth that a change of venue can alter the effects of love. Her confidence was in the principle of the family redeemer found in the Word of God. Hence, she put her faith in the law of her new and growing faith. As the near relative, Boaz could rescue Elimelech's family property that he mortgaged in order to take his family to Moab. Although

Naomi had been married to Elimelech, she did not have the money to redeem the land. But Boaz could buy it back and keep the property in the family.

In addition to the land, the wife of the deceased was a part of the family property. Therefore, the family redeemer had to marry the wife and rear the children who bore the name of the deceased. The redeemed family would inherit the property, and the family name and the family possessions would continue to be theirs as if the father of the family had not died. This was known as the "levirate marriage." The word *levir* is a Latin word which means "the husband's brother" (Deut. 25:5–10). The book of Ruth does not tell how Ruth's husband Mahlon was connected to the property. But we may assume that because this was his son and Ruth was Elimelech's daughter-in-law, she became part of the family property. This was the way of the Jewish world that this Moabite woman was now a part of.

Some cultures remain committed to caring for their wounded. One group that practices the pattern of the family redeemer is the Filipinos. To understand this is to accept the centrality of the family. The typical Filipino exists foremost as a member of a family and looks to the family as the only reliable protection against the uncertainties of life.

Members of an Oriental family rely on one another for love, support, and refuge. This has historically been as much an economic necessity as it is a cultural tradition. The relationship to family is not just a practical trade-off of autonomy for social security; concern for the welfare of the family is expressed in the respect for the older relatives and the provision offered in caring for the children, and the individual sacrifices that are made on behalf of the family members (Okamura and Agbayani, 1991).

"A Filipina, for example, can walk into a store to buy a blouse for herself and come out with one for her sister instead. The Asian family living in the United States will routinely send money, clothes, household goods, and other items as well as bring many gifts on personal visits to extended family members left behind in the Philippines" (Gochenour, 1990).

Families today could do more to secure help for the members of their clan who fall on hard times. Caring for those who have fallen on hard times is the mandate for the family: "Give proper recognition to those widows who are really in need. But if a widow has children or grandchildren, these should learn first of all to put their religion into practice by caring for their own family and so repaying their parents and grandparents, for this is pleasing to God" (1 Tim. 5:3–4).

Supporting the family is a reflection of God's caring for His own creation. As God's family, we are to emulate God's compassion toward one another, especially in regard to the family. The family in our modern society is neglected because of the high value placed on being an individual. Some people within the family are driven with becoming their own person at the risk of neglecting the clan that has nurtured them. This departing, forgetting, and abandoning is often heard of by high-profile personalities who ascertain the American dream and forget the family unit that sacrificed for their achievements.

The family that refuses to help one another in the cold, cruel world rarely benefits in the long run. The world is a cruel place, and going it alone is virtually impossible. The family is a blanket of warmth against the bitter cold and a refuge against the unsavory people we encounter. The good of the family cannot be sacrificed for a life of isolation or separation.

Ruth Lives with Her Mother-in-Law

Life goes on! God is the interlude in Ruth's journey. That is the gospel—to know that during the down times in life, God is involved in my affairs. Like the stage director giving instructions on changing the props, God is with us managing our interludes. There is nothing quiet about God during the high points of Ruth's drama. Although God often works in silence, He is constantly at work. As we near the end of another episode in Ruth's saga, it appears that nothing is resolved.

Everyone knows something about interludes. They are not relegated to any specific person or persons. From our infancy to maturity, life is a series of interludes. The duration of life is a series of starts and stops. During these times we need to catch our breath when running hard, fast, and long around life's track. The good news is we can find that rest in Jesus Christ: "Come to me, all you who are weary and burdened, and I will give you rest. Take my yoke upon you and learn from me, for I am gentle and humble in heart, and you will find rest for your souls. For my yoke is easy and my burden is light" (Matt. 11:28–30). Consider these positive points about life in the interlude the next time you are faced with a difficult choice.

Remember that God is in charge: We have a kinsman-redeemer. Christ has purchased our salvation and established a fellowship with the eternal God. Additionally, Jesus has delivered us from the interludes that come in life. "In the same way, the Spirit helps us in our weakness. We do not know what we ought to pray for, but the Spirit himself intercedes for us with groans that words cannot express" (Rom. 8:26).

To know that we have a kinsman-redeemer is marvelous, but to know that God is in charge is superb. Why? Because the kinsman-redeemer accomplishes the purposes of Yahweh. The family redeemer operates beneath the will of the Almighty. Imagine Ruth's discovery of God being in control of all her affairs. Nothing had happened by chance. Everything in Ruth and Naomi's pilgrimage toward God's plan was predetermined. Initially Ruth could not explain the strange ways of Naomi's God. Respectfully, Ruth pledged her obedience to Yahweh. During the interludes, Ruth learned that God was neither absent nor detached. The Lord always has His hands on the steering wheel. God is always moving each person to the proper place at the right time.

Remember that God is in charge: You have learned the art of living through the hard times. Ruth and Naomi knew personally what hard times are all about. Many people talk about hard times vicariously. They live their lives through the experiences of other people. These women open the windows of their souls and say, "Take a look into our world and join us in this exhilarating adventure."

There is an art to survival. Ruth and Naomi weave a mosaic for us to muse upon. They seem to speak demonstratively about life through the hard times with integrity: "The LORD gave and the LORD has taken away; may the name of the LORD be praised" (Job 1:21). Ruth and Naomi had rehearsed the speech of another fellow struggler named Job, who was faced with hard times. Ruth, Naomi, and Job ate the stale slices of bread in the hard times of life. Just because the bread isn't fresh doesn't mean it lacks nutrients.

Difficulties shape our faith. Many people would not believe as deeply as they do if it were not for adversity. An obstinate experience can push us to dependence on God. There is a scene in James Baldwin's book, *Blues for Mr. Charlie,* where the grandson goes to New York City and discovers there is no God. His discovery brings him back home and face to face with his Christian grandmother. Impetuously, he declares to Big Momma that there is no God. She replies, "Sure there is." Agitated, he protests. While in the Big Apple, he says, "I've read books and I have determined that accepting there is a God is sophomoric." Unmoved by his expanding vocabulary, Big Momma says, "Sure you do . . . just hold your breath." The breath of life will scream to be released from the lungs that pulsate to keep you alive.

Remember that God is in charge. We know this because of His providence. The title of Reform theologian R. C. Sproul's book identifies providence as *The Invisible Hand of God.* Providence isn't in vogue these days. Understanding providence is essential to appreciating God at work in your private world. Maybe you disagree with God about where you are. Then read the words of Ralph Waldo Emerson in his essays on self reliance: "Accept the place the divine providence has found for you." It's impossible to accept providence as a gift of God and be self-reliant. Independence diminishes when you embrace the leadership of the Holy Spirit. Providence connects you to the will of God. "And we know that in all things God works for the good of those who love him, who have been called according to his purpose" (Rom. 8:28).

Ruth and Naomi are an example of how Yahweh can move you from the funeral of Moab to the festival of Bethlehem. These two widows didn't have material abundance. But they did have love and respect for each other. They had the plus factor working for them. The poverty of the past had disappeared. The widows were facing a new set of concerns. Without a husband or children, the future of Ruth and Naomi appeared incredulous. This is an interlude.

During the intermission God remained gracious. Ruth and Naomi had come to the house of bread. The famine was lifted, and the harvest was ripe and ready for the reaping. Until the promises in your life are fulfilled, remember that you are surrounded by God's abundance. In every direction, God has left grain in the field for you to gather up. There is no need for you to starve for attention, love, or acceptance. "And my God will meet all your needs according to his glorious riches in Christ Jesus" (Phil. 4:19).

The story of Ruth and Naomi seemed stopped. So they waited. Waiting on God is our active duty while in the interlude. "I am still confident of this: I will see the goodness of the LORD in the land of the living. Wait for the LORD; be strong and take heart and wait for the LORD" (Ps. 27:13–14).

Chapter Six

The Beginning to All God Finishes

RUTH 3:1–18

The cavalier farmer of Bethlehem is in love! Boaz the mighty has fallen! He has been smitten by Ruth, the empress of Arabia. How brightly burns the flame? Fine is too weak a word to describe the ardor. Boaz! He is eager   Well, Boaz is eager to pop the question. Still there lives a single impediment . . . a huge fly in the marriage ointment. Boaz has a potential challenger. There is a nearer kinsman-redeemer than he. While he would like to swoop

Ruth off her feet, there is a man with prior swooping rights. So he says to Ruth:

> "Blessed are you of the LORD, my daughter! For you have shown more kindness at the end than at the beginning, in that you did not go after young men, whether poor or rich. And now, my daughter, do not fear. I will do for you all that you request, for all the people of my town know that you are a virtuous woman. Now it is true that I am a close relative; however, there is a relative closer than I. Stay this night, and in the morning it shall be that if he will perform the duty of a close relative for you—good; let him do it. But if he does not want to perform the duty for you, then I will perform the duty for you, as the LORD lives! Lie down until morning" (Ruth 3:10–13 NKJV).

Literature, says Thomas Carlyle, is "the fruit of the soul." It is easy to love literature, good literature, all literature. Literature captivates, enchants, and fascinates its admirers. I fancy it primarily because writers have a way of dealing with real-life issues in artistic ways. One literary device that authors use to address difficult themes is a euphemism—a soft term designed to take the edge off a hard term.

I remember my world literature professor at the university, who once lectured on the use of euphemisms. To explain the use of the term, she pointed out how people shy away from certain words that smack against propriety. "For instance," she said, "the word *death* unnerves the bereaved. Dying is a horrible experience, however you look at it. There is hardly any way to soften the harshness of the word. But in our attempt to grapple with death," she said, "we often use the euphemism 'passing away,' or 'crossed over'—'gone to be with the Lord.' It changes the hard words we cannot say to softer words we can say."

The military uses euphemisms when they develop nuclear weapons and call them "peace enhancers." The government takes away assistance to the poor and refers to it as "compensation." Or when executives get fired, the corporation calls it "downsizing."

Ruth's story contains some sweeter, more palatable euphemisms that make the heavy sexual overtones of the story more bearable. These euphemisms exist in part to protect the wily Naomi. Naomi? Wily? Read on and see. Naomi had a crafty trick up her sleeve to encourage Ruth's to abandon her timid approach to love. Naomi spurred Ruth's dawdling romance into a high-geared relationship. She stalked, schemed, and meddled into Ruth's affair. Why? Perhaps she remembered a time when she had left Bethlehem full, only to return to her people empty.

Conversely, there is dignity and nobility in her scheming. Naomi wanted to provide for Ruth. And though this is a very short story, you can imagine how much time must have passed to allow Naomi's crafty instructions to take place. Naomi encouraged Ruth to scheme with her so she could be in the right place at the right time. It seems devious. But it is the Bible, so we have only to lift our eyes to see that God is most active in all this scheming. There is nothing evil, haphazard, or happenstance about this story. It is deliberate and a pure tale of chaste love.

Naomi sidled up to Ruth and told her, "It's my desire for you to have a home, security, and above all a way of life that ends in rest." In the same breath, she moved in on Boaz, her kinsman-redeemer. At this time, he was viewed merely as her close relative and an extremely eligible bachelor. Plus, Boaz was wealthy. Boaz could provide Ruth a home, security, and even rest. In light of this Naomi gave Ruth some succinct, pushy, and sexually edgy instruction. The customs of that day for marriage are withheld from us, but they involved the obligation of marriage for all who were suspected of any sexual collusion.

Naomi's counsel focused on how to make our way in romance—counsel every person needs from time to time. Every woman needs an older, seasoned woman to help her through these difficult junctures of life. Mothers, therefore, in a sense are obligated to pass down their experiences, whether good or bad, to their daughters to guide them as they position themselves in preparing for marriage.

But let us look at the practical aspects of all this. Naomi nudged Ruth toward a relationship because in her matchmaker opinion Boaz looked like a good catch. Naomi said, "If you follow my instructions, I can show you how to get your man! It's not as difficult as it seems. I know that you've been hanging out with others who have worked for him and that you have found enjoyment gleaning in his fields. But Ruth, you could step further up the ladder of love if you wanted to. All you need to do is follow my instructions." Naomi sometimes seems like a saint and sometimes like a hussy. Her advice borders on the worldly, but it also borders on the godly.

On the day of the alleged plot, perhaps the wind blew all day. It was not a good morning for winnowing grain or for going out to harvest the barley in the fields. So as life and God would have it, the workers had to delay doing their work, and they welcomed the coming of the night. Since the workers could not go out and work in the field, they took the night off in order to wait until the wind died down so that in the winnowing of the barley the grain would not be blown away.

Word got back to Naomi that Boaz was going to be working the late shift. So Naomi told Ruth this was a good time to make her move. "Ruth," she said, "Boaz will have been working hard all day, and his muscles will be wearied by the stress of harvest. Go out and work near where Boaz works. Here's what I want you to do while he is working. Go in and bathe yourself, make yourself presentable. Daughter, I know the aloes that you normally bathe with would be odorous enough, but do a little extra—go a little further. Put on your best perfume. Yeah! Put it on, girl. Let down your hair. Get rid of that hideous bun you usually wear when you're working in the fields. Remember that peignoir you used to wear when you were married? Dig it out! Put it on! Don't be too forward, but don't be afraid to be enticing. Tempt him . . . keep your chastity . . . but tempt him!"

Ruth listened to Naomi and made some mental notes and prepared herself to enter the threshing floor. As she readied herself she hung on every word falling from the lips of her mother-in-law. Her heart was pounding as she began to act on Naomi's instructions.

She moved in compliance! Naomi had told her, "What I want you to do is walk down to where Boaz will be resting for the night. Now, Ruth, it can become rather tricky, because as you know the field hands often bring their prostitutes to the threshing floor. So be careful that you don't let Boaz be overly driven, sexually. Be sure he desires you but doesn't violate you. Be careful. If I know Boaz's men like I think I do, they'll be eating and drinking. Boaz will be right there with them. Wait until Boaz has drunk his fill and overeaten. When his heart is merry, when he gets slightly tipsy, find out exactly where he's going to lie down. Mark the spot. Once he's sound asleep go in and lift his skirt of his tunic and snuggle in with him. Lift his kilt all the way up to his waist until the lower half of his body is exposed. And then I want you to lie down. Now, this is dangerous business, Ruth, because if it's handled wrong, if either of you become so aroused you lose your self-control, you might destroy a glorious future!"

Suddenly this steamy saga becomes a tale of trust. Not only was Naomi trusting Ruth, but Naomi was also trusting Boaz, who was not privy to this conversation with her daughter-in-law. Ruth also had to trust herself, and she also had to trust the integrity of Boaz. But more than that, God stood on the balcony over Bethlehem, holding His breath, knowing each actor would carry out the plan with integrity. Within Ruth there was dread as she carried out this odd experiment proposed by her wise and wily mother-in-law.

Ruth followed Naomi's advice to the letter. When she bathed, perfumed, and dressed, she took the longest walk she had ever taken. Properly understood, there is a kind of spiritual metaphor in all this. We also ought to be cautious in how we present ourselves to the God we say we love. We ought to come before His presence, washed, perfumed, and dressed. We want God to take pleasure in looking at us. Oh, how often we are slovenly, unclean, and too casual in coming into God's presence. We must never come arrogantly into the presence of God but enter his courts in a daring way, expecting Him to show us grace. In fact, we lose the intentionality of worship when we come too casually into the presence of God.

Such intentionality belonged to Ruth as she took that long walk to Boaz's tent, as she quietly took her position. As she watched Boaz eat, she thrilled at how handsome Boaz was. Ruth feared for the success of Naomi's racy experiment. Boaz ate, drank, and lay down. Possibly you're a little nervous about this very edgy tale. But what was about to happen could never come to be without the accompaniment of God. This fear of the obscene played into the thinking of Ruth when she said, "Is this thing as scandalous as the ancestors and ancestresses in my past?"

There is nothing safe about the characters, themes, or love of God within the Bible. The Bible is God's love story. It is about real people. It's not fiction but biography. The world of the Bible is not a Disneyland fantasy. Neither can it be cosmeticized like an extreme makeover. The Bible is God's story of redemption. It is God carrying on a lover's quarrel with the world He desires to save. Therefore, the Bible does not need to be sanitized by our prudery.

When Ruth saw Boaz dozing from overeating, she prepared to make her move. She watched as Boaz lay down, and when he was sound asleep Ruth softly entered the room. Gently moving across the threshing floor, she heard Naomi's caveat, "Be careful! Don't let your love get out of control. Guard your heart on the threshing floor."

Creeping softly in, Ruth removed the skirt of Boaz. She lay down. Where did she lie? At his feet? She lay directly beside Boaz. The uncovering of his feet is just a euphemism to cover the frank reality of this high sexual drama. There he lay with his top torso covered, bottom undressed. She had her head turned away. At midnight, Boaz acted startled when he woke up and sensed a woman lying beside him in the darkness The wonder of her perfume made the night fragrant with desire. "Who are you?"

"I'm Ruth," she replied.

Ruth remembered all that Naomi had told her. Ruth took matters into her own hands. Boaz could see that he was uncovered. He quickly covered, and then she said, "Cover me and put me under your wing." We may not know what happened. Did anything happen? We don't know. But don't get nervous. The Bible from time to time is an edgy book. You and I are highly sexual people. God uses this passionate gift of sexuality to preserve His covenant. He passes the lineage of Christ down through ordinary courses of human sexuality. Many would like all the sex stories taken out of the Bible. Some really like the notion that storks just drop off babies. But with God storks are out, and honest-to-goodness sexuality is in.

Ruth came up with a tidy little euphemism of her own. "Bring me under your wing." In the Bible, wings are always symbolic of the power and protection of God. "Keep me as the apple of your eye; hide me in the shadow of your wings" (Ps. 17:8). Again the psalmist prayed, "Lord, give me protection beneath your wings" (Ps. 76). Remember, Boaz said God will bring you under his wings (Ruth 2), but now Ruth said, "I want you to bring me under your wing" (Ruth 3). I know God will protect me, but I want to know, will you take care of me too? I beg you, Boaz, cover me with your wing." Ruth's request is the same type of safety and pure love that women hope for here on earth. Genuine protection doesn't emanate from man but from men who trust in the power of God.

Jesus used Ruth's metaphor very well when he looked over Jerusalem and said, "I place you under my wings like a hen covers her chicks" (see Matt. 23:37). Ruth used this symbol of protection and power. She nestled herself under the wings of her kinsman-redeemer. Beneath Boaz's wings Ruth felt safe. Here is a truth learned from the Scripture: "God is our refuge and strength, an ever-present help in trouble" (Ps. 46:1). As children of God, we have the assurance of Yahweh's protection.

Ruth's story is a tale of security and safety. Ruth wanted the same thing every person wants. Ruth desired the blanket of safety and security—not in a material, earthly sense only but in peace and rest. Men see the home as brick and mortar. The tendency of men is to measure their worth by tangible possessions. In fact, we often match our value to what we possess. Somebody said it right, I think, that the difference between men and boys is the price of their toys. Women aren't interested in toys. How often they say, "All I want is a bit of you. That's all I want. I want a home and a sense of security."

Home is a significant word as it relates to security. Home is not to be mistaken for a house. Home is a place where hearts can meet and feel loved and secure! A place where there is little or no pressure. Home is where we meet under the wings of God.

Boaz did not take sexual advantage of Ruth. He was a godly man. Boaz said, "Blessed are you . . . for you have shown more kindness at the end than at the beginning" (v. 10). Naomi had said, "I left full and came back empty" (Ruth 3:10 NKJV). But here it is Naomi who has been fulfilling in the presence of Ruth, for she said, "Now you are empty, and

I want you to be filled." So she devised a scheme that would redeem and recover.

The dominant themes of the story are not uncovering but recovering. All of this is in reality a marriage proposal. Boaz looked at Ruth as if to say, "You are a better person than I, for if I had lifted your skirt, I'm not sure I would have tried to cover you back without taking advantage of you. You have shown me that you have more integrity than I have shown you. Now I'll do whatever you ask me to do."

Naomi proved herself a woman of high nobility. She had determined the character of Boaz a long time ago. *If Ruth is in the right place and Boaz is Elimelech's relative,* she thought, *I know how my husband dealt with me. The apple never falls far from the tree. I know that Boaz will be as kind to Ruth as Elimelech was to me.*

To read this story is to see God in it for His own reasons. There is a theological thread that holds this tale together. This is a parable of immense trust. Can Naomi trust Ruth? Can Ruth trust Boaz? Can Boaz trust God? Can God trust any of us players in the scheme of His will?

There's something at stake in this tale much larger than the marriage of Ruth to Boaz. God's eye is down the road of time fixed on a throne. God is working out His promise: "'I will put enmity between you and the woman, and between your offspring and hers; he will crush your head, and you will strike his heel.' To the woman he said, 'I will greatly increase your pains in childbearing; with pain you will give birth to children. Your desire will be for your husband, and he will rule over you'" (Gen. 3:15–16). God is unraveling the promise of recovery, as well as extending the seed of Abraham.

The way Yahweh will accomplish this is to cross cultures and bring Ruth and Boaz together. Their coming together will produce a son named Obed. He will have a son named Jesse. From the loins of Jesse will came a son named David, and David will be in the lineage of the coming Messiah. There's more to this tale than mere sexual intrigue—the coming of God's Anointed One. The deliverance of man from sin is at risk.

In this story, God is saying to a lost world, "Get ready for redemption! I have initiated a plan to get my Son to planet Earth because if I don't, humanity will be lost. Also, I have to deal with more than the scandal of humanity. I've got a Son to introduce to the world."

I suspect that some people wish God had used a more Sunday school methodology to pull off the incarnation, but He didn't. God is not always a neat, tidy God. God is not a domesticated deity. You cannot tame God into country club manners and dress Him in blue for communion. The cross proves that you can nail Jesus down but only if He agrees to it. God is full of surprises, and this is one of the biggest surprises in the Bible: God is going to use a Gentile, a foreigner, so she could be married into a Jewish household. That's how God got His Son on earth.

When Boaz married Ruth, God made it clear that nobody stands on the outside of history with no ethnic significance. According to God, "you are a chosen people, a royal priesthood, a holy nation, a people belonging to God, that you may declare the praises of him who called you out of darkness into his marvelous light. Once you were not a people, but now you are the people of God; once you had not received mercy, but now you have received mercy" (1 Pet. 2:9–10). There's nobody beyond God's reach. Jehovah will use anybody and everybody to protect the household of faith.

But let us examine the deepest intricacies of this story.

Boaz said to Ruth, "Stay here. There is another relative who's closer to Naomi than I am. As her kinsman-redeemer, he has the first right to marry Ruth. But if your kinsman-redeemer doesn't exercise his right of seniority, I'll be more than happy to take his lost fortunes as my own."

One wonders if Ruth's midnight temptation had not happened, would Boaz have been interested in Ruth? Some scholars say Ruth probably only showed just a little of her calf, just a little above the knee, and the story is not as sultry as we make it. But Boaz seemed to be pretty "turned on," and his "turn on" was more than theological. We can almost hear him cry, "Whoa girl! Douse that fire! I hope your priority kinsman doesn't redeem you, because I want you."

I think Boaz had a very active prayer life. "Lord, Lord, Lord, Lord, don't let my relative get as steamed up as I am." Yet Boaz never violated Ruth. When he finally counseled her, "Get up and go on home. I don't want anyone seeing you coming out of my tent at this ungodly hour of the morning," he was trying to preserve the virtue of Ruth. He wanted to safeguard her reputation.

Morning came as Ruth prepared to leave. But she came empty and she went away full because Boaz said, "Take this back with you." He gave her six ephahs of barley. Remember, earlier in the story she left with one ephah, or four gallons. Her prospects were looking up! One night by the kilt of Boaz, and she is one well-enfranchised woman. She left with twenty-four gallons.

"Take this," said Boaz. "Give me the shawl that you wear and put the barley in it."

"I can't pack all this," Ruth replied.

"Don't worry about it, just take what you can. That'll be my guarantee that you'll come back."

When Ruth got back home, Naomi asked, "Is that you, Ruth?"

"Yes."

"What happened?"

"Well, he gave me barley." Ruth didn't have to say anything else.

Naomi smiled broadly. Being a wily mother-in-law has its rewards. "Now sweetie, you've done well for one night. Go on and go to bed."

"You haven't let me finish."

"Don't have to. I know what it means. A man's a man, and sometimes God uses his manliness. It's one of those things that runs in Elimelech's clan. Let's just wait here until God works it all out."

The story of Ruth is charitable because it is so cosmic in its symbolism. It's a tale of God's beginning effort to bring His Son to planet Earth for our redemption, to buy us back to Himself. God cares about our broken world. In our fragmented world, it is God who comes to uncover, recover, and redeem. He takes the fragmented pieces of human history and synergizes them with a mosaic of healing.

My sister, Jeanella, loves jigsaw puzzles and can fit them together like nobody's business. I've always resented her a bit because I never could do puzzles well. She went overboard with jigsaw puzzles. She would buy puzzles of 500, 1000, or even 2,500 pieces. Because I couldn't work them, I asked her, "How do you put puzzles together?" And she said, "Well, I always start with the borders. I keep the picture box in front of me and start with the borders. Once I find the borders, I begin connecting the rest of the pieces. From there I move in for the kill until the middle is all done."

I can remember one puzzle painting I couldn't disentangle. It was unique. It was a puzzle of the world, but on the box they had some word like "mystery." I thought to myself, *What's so mysterious about putting a picture of the world together?* But Jeanella stayed at it, and before long she had the puzzle put together! Jeanella had put it together on a glass table. The box had not lied. There was a mystery to it. When it was complete she was so excited. I couldn't imagine why. Then she said to me, "Get under the table and look up."

I protested, "I will not . . . that's silly! Come on, Dee Dee."

"Go on," she insisted, "get under the table and look up." Reluctantly I got under the table. I looked up and to my amazement, on the reverse of the puzzle was the face of Christ. She said, "Do you know what it means?"

"Not exactly," I said. "Does it mean you got two puzzles for the price of one?"

"No, it means that it is Christ who holds the world together."

Ruth is not so grand a puzzle as we thought. Ruth never knew it, but on the underside of her wild engagement emerged the mystery of the incarnation. Ruth must have known that it is God who holds this world together. Her words are prophecy, "Your God will be my God."

Jesus' coming into the world was not by chance. From the very beginning God had a plan for the world's redemption. Just like Ruth and Boaz, God would use a virgin named Mary and an unsuspecting man named Joseph. Moreover, God would get in the mix of the miracle. God said to the fearful heart of Joseph, "Do not be afraid to take Mary home as your wife, because what is conceived in her is from the Holy Spirit. She will give birth to a son, and you are to give him the name Jesus, because he will save his people from their sins" (Matt. 1:20–21).

The Bible is not a safe book to read. Biblical narratives are full of twists, turns, and surprises. The tale of Ruth is not a safe little story! So don't read the Bible unless you want to be challenged or changed. God is not interested in preserving our little human niceties. God has a larger world at stake. He has a world that He's trying to put together, to reconcile back to Himself so the people who live within it can become all God has called them to be. And when the pieces of your life are all assembled, and if the pieces are of God's origin, you too will see on the back side of your scrambled portrait the face of Christ.

Chapter Seven

A Good Faith
Transaction

RUTH 4:1–12

The ultimate words stamped across of our obedience may be, "Let God be God." The phrase
calls heaven to attention and makes it clear that
we are ready to take our hands off all those affairs
we have tried to manage on our own. In effect we
are saying, "Let go and let God" because we're not
doing well with the job.

Boaz could hardly wait to get into the city
square where the people would assemble at the gate
where business transactions took place. The city

square was the equivalent of the city courthouse in our day. Boaz was at the gates because there was a legal matter he needed to take care of after his long, intriguing night with Ruth. Boaz moved quickly. His steps were hastened by his responsibility. He knew the onus of this responsibility rested squarely on his shoulders.

> Then Boaz said, "On the day you buy
> the field from the hand of Naomi, you must
> also buy it from Ruth the Moabitess, the
> wife of the dead, to perpetuate the name of
> the dead through his inheritance." And the
> close relative said, "I cannot redeem it for
> myself, lest I ruin my own inheritance. You
> redeem my right of redemption for yourself,
> for I cannot redeem it" (Ruth 4:5–6 NKJV).

The nameless co-redeemer said initially, "I will redeem it" (v. 4). But after Boaz's intricate details pertaining to the kinsman-redeemer's obligation regarding the transaction, the kinsman said, "I cannot redeem it" (v. 6).

Earlier in the story, Ruth had said to Naomi, "Your God shall be my God." This sounds poetic and idyllic, but Ruth, like ourselves, didn't know all it means when we take our hands off our human mismanagement and say, "Let God be God." As established in previous chapters, God is no tame, lame, ever-the-same, domesticated deity. He's a

God of surprises! "For my thoughts are not your thoughts, neither are your ways my ways . . . As the heavens are higher than the earth, so are my ways higher than your ways and my thoughts than your thoughts" (Isa. 55:8–9). God is always working His will through the lives of all people. Every redemptive move on man's behalf involves human intervention. Ruth long before had made the choice to start her life over in the land of Bethlehem.

In the "House of Bread," Ruth entered a world different from her previous one. Once Ruth moved to Bethlehem she entered the fields where she met her kinsman-redeemer. Clearly, the moves encircling the life of Ruth were to fulfill God's ultimate plan. Every detail of these courageous women's lives was orchestrated by God's hands. Each move brought the remnant of this family closer to God's purpose.

So dawned that glorious morning when Boaz moved quickly to the town gates where all business took place. Boaz knew if he stayed there long enough, it would be just a matter of time before this co-redeemer passed by the gate on his way to the field. All at once Boaz's patience was rewarded. He saw the man. It was his first cousin, who had the first right of redemption for all Naomi owned. He was a close relative of the clan of Elimelech, and Boaz knew he must be bargained with according to law before Ruth could actually become his wife.

After a quick exchange and a few words of congenial catch-up, Boaz fast-forwarded to the life of Naomi. Boaz challenged his cousin bluntly: "You're aware of all that has befallen our relative Naomi? After the death of Elimelech, Naomi has returned from Moab."

This nameless co-redeemer replied, "Yes, I'm aware of all that has taken place."

"You know also that Naomi's sons, Mahlon and Kilion, have died?"

"This is old news, Boaz. Why are you repeating it?"

"Because I want to bring you up to speed on what's taken place."

They sat there at the city gate and exchanged familial stories. Boaz opened the family records. They were rehashed, reopened, and revisited. Finally, Boaz delved into the critical subject at hand.

"Naomi has a piece of land," he said. Suddenly, this tale of lovers takes a surprising turn. Once again the conversation is peppered with the repetition of an old woman's emptiness. Earlier in our narrative, Naomi said that she left the land of bread full but returned empty, implying she had not only lost her husband and sons, but everything. Now there is a new piece of evidence that Naomi had not quite lost everything. Naomi owned a bit of property when she left for Moab. It was hers still. Naomi was not as empty as she thought. When we lose something important there is a tendency to focus on the loss, and yet God remembers the smallest things to remind us we owe so much more than we think.

Boaz said to this cousin at the gate, "Did you know Naomi has property? It belonged to her late husband Elimelech, and Naomi is interested in selling it. You and I are her remaining relatives and nearest of kin. Legally, you are a closer relative than I. While I would like to buy it, according to law I must give you the first right of refusal."

Boaz served as a sort of realtor to make sure the property was sold and in a strictly legal manner. He spoke in direct business-like terms. Boaz appeared to be speaking on behalf of Naomi, but we know something this nameless co-redeemer could never guess. He was a mere pawn on the chessboard of life. God was working beyond Boaz's need to buy or sell property. The property must be redeemed for the welfare of Israel and the history of the Messiah.

God may not be in full view on the surface of this story, but behind the scenes God always works world history to His own ends. The central idea of this text's teaching is that God is always accountable for the future welfare of His people. We sin against our own security when we think we have to hold all responsibility of life ourselves. We grow too arrogant when we feel we have to grind at life daily to make our lives work. We do not have to dig through life all by ourselves. There is a God who holds Himself responsible for the welfare of His children.

In the tale of Ruth, a great deal is on the table. A piece of land must be sold. It's a good piece of land in a good place. On this land there are great barley fields, yielding great harvests. In this deal there are big threshing floors and a lot of money to be made. You may be sure Boaz's co-redeemer listened intently.

Boaz kept pushing the man, "If you don't take care of it to redeem it, then the welfare of Naomi is left open-ended. Who knows what may become of Naomi and her kinsman-redeemer. You must take care of these business responsibilities. They belong to you as her next of kin."

"Yes, I have no problem with doing that. That's exactly what I'll do. I'll make sure everything is done. I want to preserve the legacy of my relative. Naomi is my family, and family is very important. Let me handle all of the contractual details in order to secure Naomi's future."

Boaz wanted to make sure the legal issue was settled. He knew this "next of kin" shyster might buy the land and actually not take care of Naomi, or he could take care of Naomi without really taking care of the land.

Boaz knew that Naomi had been through enough. Three graves loomed in the backdrop. Names were given to these graves: Elimelech, Mahlon, and Kilion. Boaz had an eager interest in doing both what was right and what was loving. Everybody is named in this story except the nearest of kin. The storyteller knew the next of kin was making only a cameo appearance. He was on and off the stage of Israeli history very quickly. At the central part of the unfolding drama, he dominated the transaction at the present moment.

Redemption is the real word here! To redeem means to buy back. During a dark period in human history, humans were sold from the auction block to persons willing to pay big sums of money. The purchase guaranteed the ownership of these slaves. Sometimes purchasing these slaves resulted in their freedom. By paying the price for these help-less humans they were redeemed, and often they pledged their undying loyalty to the person who paid for their freedom. Their freedom was bought with a price. And redemption is what Boaz was after. He was after the purchase and restoration of something precious. Boaz said, "I will redeem it."

What really takes place in this story? Elimelech was gone, and yet his land and family in Hebrew thought were forever a part of his legacy. Caring for a man's family and purchasing his land were considered the enduring right of the family. It was somehow more than legal; it was a "good faith" transaction. Boaz ended his business proposal by saying, "Naomi is not just selling her property." He was saying to the nearest kinsman-redeemer, "Purchase this for Naomi's redemption so she can be cared for."

The nearer kinsman-redeemer seemed willing to own the property but not to care for the women. Boaz made it clear: "When you buy the land and redeem it, you're also inheriting the care and upkeep of Naomi and her daughter-in-law, Ruth, Mahlon's widow. Also, you will have to conceive a child by this daughter-in-law, and the child who is born will become Naomi's grandchild. Then you will have to relinquish your investments of your family to care for these women and the child."

Boaz was wealthy and probably was better off financially than this co-redeemer. Perhaps Boaz's solvency caused the co-redeemer to back away from trying to "out-bargain" a man of means. Boaz did not give all the facts. Had Boaz been altogether up front, he might have said, "One reason you think you don't want to purchase the property and Ruth is because you haven't seen Ruth. If you had seen Ruth, you would not be jumping to the conclusion and saying, 'I can't do that.' In fact, you would sell every barley field you have just to get the woman if you knew what I know about Ruth."

Jesus said the "kingdom of heaven is like treasure hidden in a field. When a man found it, he hid it again, and then in his joy went and sold all he had and bought that field" (Matt. 13:44). In order to purchase the hidden treasure, the finder sold everything to own it. To own the treasure is to experience the joy of heaven. Boaz went to extreme measures to secure the riches of Ruth's affection.

Boaz was a shrewd negotiator. He didn't exactly lie, but he used "creative ethics." He wasn't lying; he was just using limited evidence to sweeten his end of the bargain.

What's to be said of law and creative ethics? The symbol of "Lady Justice" is blind, and she holds a set of scales in her hands. She can't see what's on the balances and which side weighs heaviest. The balance she holds says everything has to be done equally. Good and fair justice says, "You are innocent until proven guilty." Many of us know equality doesn't always hold true. Justice may be blind, but God is not.

When God broaches the subject of redemption, He does not enter negotiation blindfolded. God actually knows every intricate detail of our beings, and yet He is still willing to send a Redeemer to purchase our redemption. Initially, this truth pertaining to redemption might appear bland. On the other hand, it is most exciting to know God sees and knows everything about us and is still willing to spend the life of his Son to purchase our redemption. This is the loftiest miracle of the New Testament.

The greatest miracle of the New Testament is not merely that Jesus Christ, the ultimate Redeemer, would die in our place and buy us back for God. The greatest miracle of the New Testament is God being willing to purchase back what He owns—what He has always owned. It would be one thing for God to redeem someone if He didn't have all the evidence—if all the facts had not been turned in. But the miracle of the New Testament is that God is willing to die for all of us when the Gracious One knows every detail of our conscience and morality. God knows we have missed the mark. God knows we have stumbled. The Eternal knows where we fall. God knows that we have erred. With all of the evidence stacked against us, God was still willing to send His Son Jesus to die for us.

God loves us in spite of who we are. Anybody who is married certainly understands such second-hand forgiveness. To love for a lifetime is to understand the flaws in our marriage companion and to go on loving him or her anyway. To love is to stay married to a person even when you know his or her Achilles' heel. To love them is to know where they need to retouch the photograph of their lives. It is to know their scars, marks, and blemishes. It is to know they do not always talk in private the way they do in public. It is to see they're not always as courteous in private as they are in public. Yet the glory of the relationship is to cherish marriage because love has a unique tendency of covering the multitude of blemishes we find in each other.

All parents know something about this. Parents know their children are not always all they say they are on the public stage. They are not always what they appear to be in those beautiful baby pictures. But we do not cast them out of the family. We do not throw them away. There is something about redeeming love that always says, "I love you enough to stay the course with you." So maintain! Hold on! Keep at it! We must serve our mates and families the way God serves us. We want to be redemptive and loving because God is. Redemption comes because God loves us enough to hold on to the entities that He has a right to throw away.

Redemption is the role of the kinsman-redeemer. The redeemer buys back property which he knows was lost but was of great value. Boaz said to the would-be redeemer, "I wanted to make sure I shared that piece of information with you because if you're not going to redeem this precious widow and her daughter-in-law, then I'll redeem them." Then Boaz said to the elders around him, "In this market square, I want us to sign the contract."

In those days, "business partners" did not pull out a pen and sign on the dotted line. Back then, the legal seal came when the sandals were taken off.

When the sandals came off, there was an exchange of the Levitical law. All agreed on what had been negotiated. Then the sandal was given in pledge. This odd ritual was the marker of a good-faith transaction. The land and the women were turned over to Boaz. Boaz called the witnesses and said, "You have seen with your own eyes what has taken place here. Are we in agreement this is the transaction that shall occur?"

"Yes, this is it," they said.

"Fine."

Here the story ends almost too abruptly. Still the writer issues a kind of reporting that synchronizes the transaction. It begins to call up both by playing up some names like Rachel, Leah, and Tamar. Leah in some ways was hardly a beauty, and Tamar was certainly scandalous because she preserved the lineage of her family by seducing her drunken father-in-law. Rachel was beautiful. Leah, her sister, had a crooked eye. But alongside this gathering of princesses and non-princesses was Ruth, the Moabitess. The names of all these women show up in the lineage of Jesus. You would think that if Jesus could have picked His ancestors, He would have picked some better ones than this. When God put the lineage of Jesus together, He incorporated not only scandalous women but a few masculine rascals as well.

Why? God does it for people like us. I don't know your sin or sense of need for Christ. But I know mine. God did all of this for Ralph West. We don't boast about sin. Neither are we to brag about iniquity. We are not proud of transgressions. We have blemishes and moral scars. Don't mistake this as a promotion of anyone's error and failure, certainly not my own. The redeemed are guilty of many wrong things. "All have sinned and fall short of the glory of God" (Rom. 3:23). If God had not put these rogues in the lineage of Jesus, we would never have been able to live up to His standards.

Interestingly, the people who appear in Jesus' lineage are the same types of people who show up in the church. Consider Jesus' grandmothers, Ruth, Bathsheba, and Leah, not to mention Jesus' great-great-great grandmamma, Rahab. God added these folk in the family lineage to remind us that God's grace has no limits.

Grace and redemption pass no one by. Many people are carrying a massive load of guilt and actually feel as if their lives are beyond God's reach. They would like a good-faith negotiation with God, but they feel they are beyond redemption. They swelter under the details of the mistakes they have made and the errors they have committed. They seem to act as though this is something new to the blindfolded eyes of God. But remember, God says, "Before you were ever born, in your mother's womb, I knew you. All have missed the mark I have set before you. There is no one beyond My redemption. You can't fall so low that I can't lift you."

You may need redemption so desperately that you feel whatever you have broken cannot be mended. You may even feel that God has turned His back on you. You may ask like the psalmist, "My God, my God, why have you forsaken me? Why are you so far from saving me, so far from the words of my groaning?" (Ps. 22:1).

Despair not!

You have a kinsman-redeemer! His name is Jesus. Jesus Christ has already taken on Himself all of the sins you will ever commit. Jesus has nailed those sins to the cross so you could be bought back. Jesus has taken His sandals off at the cross—His good-faith transaction is complete. Jesus has offered His naked feet to the nails. You have been bought!

I remember merchants with whom our family traded gave out spending perks called Green Stamps. Our family (and almost all others) kept Green Stamp books where we pasted in the stamps. When we collected enough Green Stamps, we could take our books of stamps into the S&H Green Stamp redemption center and trade them in for the merchandise of our dreams. What you wanted to purchase with these stamp books dictated how many little Green Stamp books you needed. All of us took our books into the redemption center to exchange our Green Stamps for the products we wanted to purchase. In other words, we purchased our "dream" products through redemption.

It was a good-faith transaction.

God knew not only that Mahlon's lineage needed to be preserved but also that Boaz's lineage, which was his propagation, should also not be blotted out of the family records.

God knew our names couldn't even be put in the book of life until He had first exchanged our salvation with Christ's blood at heaven's grand redemption center. What God actually does in redemption is to say, "This is My Son whom I offer up so I can get My child back into My possession." Let me be more specific. On Good Friday God said, "Here's Jesus; now give Me Ralph West." Or you can put your name in the blank. That's what God does in purchasing our redemption.

Perhaps you are thinking, *But I'm not worthy.* Indeed, you are not. Who is? Obed wasn't worthy. Ruth wasn't worthy. Boaz wasn't worthy. You're not worthy. I'm not worthy. But heaven has never been based on our worthiness but on the Word of God. This is the miracle of Christianity. God is willing to die for what we know has been devalued by our sin. And yet in redemption, God, in His good-faith transaction, says that He is going to purchase us with a price greater than our worth. Sin has marred and scarred us, but He is going to pay the perfect price and offer us a perfect redemption.

The story of Boaz and Ruth moves to a swift conclusion. No longer does Ruth have to risk her reputation by lying at the feet of Boaz. Now, the pair has conceived a child. But when the child is born they call this baby Naomi's baby. Naomi becomes the baby's nurse. This baby brings joy and laughter into the lives of Naomi, Ruth, and Boaz.

The latter part of the story belongs to Naomi to remind us of one last thing. Vanished, gone is her former bitter soul. Naomi's testimony from her initial return was, "I left full, but I came back empty." Naomi is a nurse for Ruth and Boaz's baby. The scandal of emptiness has been erased. Naomi, according to Ruth's tale, will never know disappointment again.

Life has a way of emptying us. There are those among us who wonder, *How did I get to the deplorable state I find myself in? How did it happen? What went wrong? How did I get so empty? How did I become so bitter? I used to be such an upbeat, joyful person.*

God gives us back our lives in a way only God can give. Howard Thurman says, "Anything that is against God is against life." That which is against life is against God. Here is why it's so important for all of us to treat people as family and not as adjectives. We must in good faith love one another as God loves us.

To be brought back is to stop whipping ourselves down for the mistakes we have made. God in redemption makes everything new. That is what redemption does. It brings a sense of newness. God "has made everything beautiful in its time. He has also set eternity in the hearts of men; yet they cannot fathom what God has done from beginning to end" (Eccl. 3:11). In redeeming us God actually gives us a place to start all over. This is why forgiveness and redemption are first cousins. In forgiveness God cleans up the slate.

Sometimes the church is the last place in the world to look for forgiveness. It is incredible how hard it is for us to forgive people today. It is difficult to forgive up close, to forgive the person sitting next to you, or the person living in the same house. The offenders as well as the offended need the gift of forgiveness. We need forgiveness because it releases us from the guilt, shame, and hurt we inflict on ourselves. All of us have enough baggage and sin to land us in hell if it were not for the redemption of Jesus Christ. The only reason we are here is because of grace and mercy. We're here because God has redeemed us, filling our emptiness with the fullness of Christ.

So that is what redemption does. Look at Naomi holding baby Obed. This gives you the sense of a brand-new start in life. It is such a life God offers you through Christ. Grace is God's good-faith transaction for you.

So move out of your old, decrepit mind-set into a new dynamic posture. Let the old things pass away. Let everything that God wants for you become new. Let the world know you are God's partner in a good-faith transaction.

Thus, the book of Ruth ends. It ends in what appears a strange way. The last few lines seem like a dull appendix to a very exciting book: "This, then, is the family line of Perez: Perez was the father of Hezron, Hezron the father of Ram, Ram the father of Amminadab, Amminadab the father of Nahshon, Nahshon the father of Salmon, Salmon the father of Boaz, Boaz the father of Obed, Obed the father of Jesse, and Jesse the father of David" (Ruth 4:18–22). This seemingly dull genealogy holds a fire-burst of glory! From the lineage of David comes God's final great Kinsman-Redeemer! His name is Jesus.

Chapter Eight

The Long, Long Corridors of Obedience

Ruth 4:13–22

Gordon MacDonald in his book *Ordering Your Private World* remembers "the sadness of a book never read." While he and his wife Gail were browsing in an old bookstore, they came across a copy of Daniel Webster's biography published in the 1840s. Being lovers of biographies, they purchased the book. The book cover was worn and the book appeared to be well read. Apparently the book was a prized possession of some New England family. He imagined the book had provided enlightenment to many different readers.

But this was not the case! The publisher's printer had cut the book pages improperly. Many of the pages could not be opened without the assistance of a knife to cut them apart. The uncut pages were clear evidence that the book had never been read! On the outside the book appeared to have been constantly used. Probably the book was used as a doorstop or perhaps a booster for a child to sit on at the table. Maybe Webster's biography had occupied space only in some gracious library. The book may have been used, but it certainly had never been read.

There's a tragedy in a book left unread. To read part of a biography and stop midway is the equivalent to meeting half a person. The purpose of reading the entire biography is to become acquainted with the life and experiences of a person. Likewise, to read the story of Ruth and stop at the birth of a baby is to end the narrative prematurely. To end the tale at the birth without the inclusion of the "genealogy of David" is to miss the primary purpose of this love story. The names in the family listing are often overlooked as inconsequential. Not so! These names are the key to unlocking our understanding of the Messiah's arrival.

The Danish philosopher Søren Kierkegaard said, "Life must be lived forward but it can only be understood by looking backwards." An acquaintance said to me, "If hindsight could be sold, everyone would be rich." Looking backwards down the long corridors of obedience, every intricate detail in the lives of Naomi and Ruth is falling into place. Although Elimelech's initial move bordered on disobedience, the reader is reminded that God is in charge. The famine is why Elimelech relocated his family to Moab. In this alien territory Mahlon and Kilion married women racially different from their mother. But they were told not to pay attention to these girls' race but to give credence to their character.

Quickly the wedding chimes are exchanged for the tolling bells of a funeral. The bitterness of Moab is expressed in the death of Elimelech, Mahlon, and Kilion. A family full of life is quickly reduced to emptiness and a dismal future. Naomi's need to return home, Orpah's desire to remain in her country, and Ruth's determination to accompany her mother-in-law make for high drama. The fields of Bethlehem and the leftover stalks are provisions made by Yahweh but unknown to Ruth.

The chance meeting with Boaz is all a part of the scheme of Yahweh. Naomi's seduction tempered with chastity allures Boaz, and he is also a pawn in the hands of God. Finally the bitterness of Moab is replaced with new joy found in Bethlehem. The lives of Naomi and Ruth, two trusting women, whose lives were marked by famine and funerals, are compensated by the birth of a baby into the family.

Boaz has honored Ruth's request, "Spread the corner of your garment over me, since you are a kinsman-redeemer" (Ruth 3:9). He has placed Ruth beneath the protection of his wings. The two are nestled down in their new home. The waiting is over, and lovemaking can begin. After Boaz made Ruth his wife, "The LORD enabled her to conceive, and she gave birth to a son" (Ruth 4:13). A son is born to take away the misery of the sons of Naomi who died in the land of Moab. New life can begin. The birth of the baby reminds us that only God can sanction life. "I have come that they may have life, and have it to the full" (John 10:10).

In the meanwhile, Naomi is at home enjoying her redeemed life when suddenly neighboring women break in on her tranquillity. The same women we met earlier in the narrative singing the funeral dirge of emptiness now change their song to "happy days are here again." Their merriment fills the air with jubilation. The house is filled with excitement. The women are unaware of the accuracy of their praise. "Praise be to the LORD, who this day has not left you without a kinsman-redeemer" (Ruth 4:14).

According to their praise, it is the Lord who is at work behind the scenes in the life of Naomi and Ruth. Yahweh has provided the newborn. Robert Hubbard, Jr. says, "Coming as it does at the story's end, however, the reference may be to all the events which led to the child's provision, not just to the birth itself . . . the widow's return, the chance meeting, the successful scheme, and the day in court." Everything has Yahweh's fingerprints on it. Nothing has happened to Naomi or Ruth without the permission of God's sovereignty.

The women reporting this grand surprise place the baby in the lap of Naomi. "Blessed be the LORD," they say, "who has not left you this day without next of kin" (Ruth 4:14 RSV). Herein is the purpose of the child's birth. God once again has provided for the future of Naomi. This is the last time the story uses the term *redeemer.* But it is certainly not the last time God will redeem. Is the redeemer Boaz? Is it the child? Or is it perhaps God? It is God after all who has come to redeem what belongs to Him. It is God who is the protagonist of this story. As in all stories God incorporates people to accomplish His purpose. God uses a child to secure the posterity of Elimelech's family.

The women continue in their exhortation: "May [the baby] become famous throughout Israel!" (Ruth 4:14). The women add a prayer to their praise for the infant to become famous, just as the men prayed for the same thing for Boaz (Ruth 4:11). The hope is for the child's fame to exceed the father's sterling reputation, extending beyond Bethlehem to the entire nation of Israel. Here we can truly say, "Like father like son."

The child is a gift from God, and the women are eager to mention the benefits Naomi is to enjoy. The baby will "renew your life" (Ruth 4:15). Moreover, the kinsman will give Naomi a renewed life. Forever the two women will have their needs met. The baby is the security for the family. This is the real kinsman-redeemer.

In Naomi's graying years, "she will be sustained." The love of Ruth for her mother-in-law shines through this story, and it is appropriate that it is given recognition at the end. The recognition of Ruth's gift is seen as being "better . . . than seven sons" (Ruth 4:15). Naomi's daughter-in-law loves her mother. The love of Ruth is witnessed by her surrendering her son and giving him to Naomi as her own child. It is striking, given the place of boys in comparison to girls. To have several male progeny was the supreme gift to married people. To speak of Ruth as being more valuable than seven sons was the highest honor she could receive. Seven sons was the proverbial portrait of the perfect family (1 Sam. 2:5).

The women carried the infant from the honeymoon suite of Ruth and Boaz to the hamlet of

Naomi. Once the women were in the company of Naomi, they handed the baby to his foster mother. The empty Naomi realized her final fulfillment. She was full for the first time and ready to start life over again. As she took the baby into her care, she laid him on her breast. The newborn snuggled in the arms of gray-haired Naomi! It had been a long, lonely walk down the corridors of obedience for this mother. Death took away Naomi's motherhood, but her daughter-in-law had given it back to her again.

The women said, "Naomi has a son" (Ruth 4:17). What shall we name the baby? One of the women suggest the name Obed! That's a good strong, responsible name. What does his name mean? It means literally, "One who works or one who serves." Obed's name carries more meaning than any of the women or Naomi can imagine. Obed will work and serve Naomi. He will provide food for her and take care of her in her graying years. Naomi will never have to worry about daily provisions as long as her "servant" is around.

Good thing we didn't stop the story before we got to the naming of the child. We would have missed a significant part of the story. Obed is essential to our understanding of the coming Messiah. Obed's name may scarcely be mentioned when we talk about the Messiah, but without him there would be no Jesse. Here again is an important name for our understanding of the Anointed One.

The succinct genealogy introduces us to the future king of Israel. Obed "was the father of Jesse, the father of David" (Ruth 4:17). This line supplies more information about our birth child Obed, who happens to be the grandfather of Israel's revered King David. Now this simple love story of two struggling women reveals new dimensions. Obed will serve a greater purpose—the will of God. From the beginning God has planned to come to His people on human terms. For Ruth, this was the crowning event of her strange but exciting saga. Who would have forecast such a destiny for a Moabite immigrant! With what generosity Yahweh rewards those who seek refuge under His wings!

In order to accomplish this venture, God used some interesting people. The key players in God's project of incarnation lack outstanding visible presence in the Bible. These characters and roles they play are significant to the future of Israel. But they make only cameo appearances at best. In other words, only composite sketches are available for some of these figures. On the other hand, a plethora of biographical material is available on others. Nevertheless, each person is essential for the coming of the Messiah.

Consider Jesse. What we know about him is miniscule, but without him the great poet-warrior

David would not exist. We know that Jesse was the son of Obed and the father of David. He was the grandson of Boaz and Ruth and an ancestor of Christ (Ruth 4:17, 22). His name means "Jehovah is firm." We know Jesse was the father of eight sons (1 Sam. 17:12–14). Jesse was a man of no rank who lived in Bethlehem and worked as a shepherd. The prophet Isaiah said about him, "A shoot will come up from the stump of Jesse; from his roots a Branch will bear fruit" (Isa. 11:1). The prophet indicated that the Messiah would come from Jesse. The humble ancestry of the Messiah is contrasted with the glorious kingdom He will have. When the prophet Samuel came to Bethlehem seeking the Lord's anointed, it was inconceivable that David was Yahweh's chosen servant. Most parents disbelieve when greatness is living under their roof.

There we have it, a few references here and there throughout the Scripture about Jesse. His resumé is not extensive or very impressive when you read it separate from the life of his son David. Yet Jesse is the vital link between Obed and David and ultimately Christ the Lord. Therefore, the length of a person's resumé is not what makes him important. As Peter Marshall once said, "Life is not measured by duration but by donation." Jesse donated his seed, and now we rejoice that Jesus is the Son of David, of the seed of Abraham.

Subsequently, we come to David, the son of Jesse, who is a mountain peak among Bible characters. He was chosen as Israel's second king by God Himself. David was a type for the coming of the real King of the world—Christ the Messiah. The great poet-warrior David resembled the Messiah at several points. Both David and Jesus were born in the little town of Bethlehem. Both were of low esteem on the earth. They had nothing to boast about and were the least in their family ranking. Neither David nor Jesus had wealth to commend them to the world. They were shepherds, David caring for sheep and Jesus caring for the souls of people. Both were sorely oppressed and suffered persecution, but neither opened his mouth against his detractors.

Ultimately both came to kingship. David conquered his enemies and united Judah and Jerusalem. His kingdom stretched from shore to shore. Jesus, on the other hand, was born a King; he came announcing the kingdom of God, thus establishing His eternal kingdom. Of His kingdom there shall be no end.

The story of Ruth tells us that our lives are bigger than any one of us can imagine. Who can know the entire scheme of his life on planet earth? "Now we see but a poor reflection as in a mirror; then we shall see face to face. Now I know in part; then I shall know fully, even as I am fully known" (1 Cor. 13:12). Our purpose of being is more than a birth date or a death date. We are a part of the long-range planning of a loving God. The aim of God has not changed; His aim is not to fulfill our goal but to achieve God's intention. God's passionate desire is to reclaim what belongs to Him.

When the Arab gleaner passed on her genes and bloodline to the Son of God, she was ignorant of the full weight of this act. Calvary was Ruth's ultimate business, and she never knew it. How could she know it, and how can we know what the highest purposes of God are? We can only know when we meet God's token for the journey of life—Jesus Christ the Anointed One. In the person of Jesus Christ our lives have more importance than we know. "For in him we live and move and have our being" (Acts 17:28). The great men and women of the Bible were unaware of their significance in the redemptive drama of God. You and I are equally unsuspecting of the ways God will use our lives for the greater unfolding of His purpose in the world today!

We can celebrate the fact that there are no insignificant people in God's story. We all play an important role in the story of redemption. Even though Jesus has already come to the world and has revealed Himself as God's Anointed One, Christ continues to perform His wonderful miracles among us. Even the church is the prolonged incarnational reality of God. It preserves His presence in the world through the power of the Holy Spirit. We can be a part of God's church and triumph victoriously even as Christ reigns as Lord.

This is the significance of the story of Ruth. This historical narrative reveals that God is redeeming His creation. The end of the story is not with the birth of Obed. The birth of Obed is only the beginning. This great love story, like all grand love stories, ends with Jesus!

Conclusion

The story of Ruth brings into focus that life can begin again. No one is exempt from experiences of loss. Eventually we come to life's juncture and ponder whether life can ever get back to normal. This is often the case when a spouse, child, or loved one dies. The emptiness leaves such an absence until the survivor grapples with the possibilities of making it through life without their significant other. Precisely at this point Ruth exposes her wounds and takes on the role of healer.

At the heart of Ruth, as well as at the center of our own story, is the much-needed but often-forgotten act of repentance. In the Christian vernacular *repentance* is almost a forgotten word. Maybe the word *repent* is endangered because it smacks as being archaic. Repentance is essential to our getting back into a right relationship with Jesus Christ. Yet the story of Ruth reeks with its relevance. The entire story is about a group of people starting over. Naomi starts over with Ruth. Next Ruth starts over with Naomi. Then Naomi and Ruth are starting over with Boaz. Then there is Boaz starting over with Ruth. And finally, Naomi, Ruth, and Boaz each start over with Obed.

Today you can include your name on the beginning-over-again list. For years, I have tried to log my spiritual journey into my journal. Too often, my personal hiatus has kept me from a consistent entry. But when I feel the urge to write I find myself paralyzed because of all the missteps I have taken since the last entry. Because of my inconsistencies I become apologetic. Read how I began each line, "Well here I go, starting over again." Once after being frustrated with my delinquencies I began by writing, *No More Starting Over.*

Maybe you feel that way. "No more starting over" is your mantra. "This time I am starting my diet, and I'm going to stick to it." Or, "I'm going to lose these twenty pounds if it's the last thing I do." "I'm going to quit smoking." Or you declare "I'm going to read my Bible and pray daily." The list can be interminable. The point is you've vowed never to start over again. Realistically it's impossible. Since you are imperfect, chances are you will start something over again and again. Therefore, stop punishing yourself over it. God has given to you the great gift of repentance. It is the joyful release of seeing yourself the way that God sees you. Surprisingly God always sees us in a better light than we see ourselves.

Seeing that starting over is a gift from the Gracious One, why not start over? Suppose we approach our day by saying, *Yes, more starting over.* This is precisely the ministry Jesus. Our Lord has come to lift us to a higher level in living. This is what he means when he says, "I have come that you might have life and have it to the full." The goal of Christian living is to have a complete life—not a life modeled after disingenuous relationships but a life full of the satisfying bread that Jesus bakes. "I am the bread of life. He who comes to me will never go hungry, and he who believes in me will never be thirsty."

Probably you have failed and made a terrible mistake. Society has disqualified you. The mark of Cain identifies you as a fugitive from God. Still there is within you the desire to start clean and put away past guilt, shame, and disgrace. This is exactly what repentance affords us, a new sheet of paper to write a grand new chapter. Make a new entry in your diary. Today I started over again with Jesus, and we are walking together. Starting over doesn't imply failure or mistake. Often beginning anew refers to different and exciting adventures of interest. Start over in your attitude. Start over in your worship. Start over in your service. Start over in your love towards God. I want to encourage you to start over and find fullness.

Well, finally we've arrived at the beginning.